RELEASING THE POWER IN FATHERHOOD

The Dynamics of Effective Fathering

FRANCIS EDO OLOTU

authorHOUSE®

AuthorHouse™
1663 Liberty Drive
Bloomington, IN 47403
www.authorhouse.com
Phone: 1-800-839-8640

First published by AuthorHouse   10/7/2009

ISBN: 978-1-4490-2333-1 (sc)

Printed in the United States of America
Bloomington, Indiana

This book is printed on acid-free paper.

ACKNOWLEDGEMENTS

I am indebted to many persons who offered ideas, suggestions and support in diverse ways to enable me achieve my goal.

Dr Isaac E. Ukpokolo wrote the foreword to this book after painstakingly reading through it.

Sr Rita Akin-Otiko took time off her busy schedule to proof-read the manuscript and offered helpful suggestions.

My daughters Ufuoma and Odiri made valuable inputs into some of the chapters of this book.

My wife Bukie gave unquantifiable moral support in writing this book and was also on-hand to proof-read the whole book. Her editorial and secretarial inputs made me finish this book on schedule.

CONTENTS

PART SEVEN: DEVELOPING CRITICAL LIFE SKILLS

PREFACE

Inside every child lies a genius waiting to be discovered; a father is both divinely appointed and uniquely positioned to unearth this genius. He does this by deploying fathering skills that transform the child.

Releasing the Power in Fatherhood was written to equip men with the technicalities of fathering. It is meant to educate, stimulate and inspire men to be better fathers by developing their fathering skills to the fullest.

Knowing that there are innate abilities that must be identified, nurtured and released in the life of every child; a father is the arrow head of the team of those who are in a position of empowering a child to attain his destiny. He does this as he adds value to his child's life by training the child and imparting skills that will empower the child to take advantage of life's chances that will come his way.

Harvard University, founded in 1636 is America's premier University that had been a leader in offering qualitative education for over 350 years. Its preadmission requirement for undergraduates demands that prospective candidates get evaluated by their previous school head or school counselor for the following character and personality traits: Intellectual curiosity, Intellectual creativity, Academic promise, Leadership, Sense of responsibility, Self-confidence, Self-reliance, Warmth of personality, Sense of humour, Integrity, Maturity, Initiative, Concern for others and Reaction to set backs etc. A candidate is required to score highly in this evaluation. A school that has produced six American Presidents i.e. John Adams, John Quincy Adams, Theodore Roosevelt, Franklin Roosevelt, John F Kennedy and Barack Obama must have noted personality and character traits of those most likely to succeed in life and so made them preadmission requirements. One thing common to all these traits is the fact that they are acquired in early life and all can be imparted by parents who are focused and have the necessary parenting skills.

Releasing the Power in Fatherhood was written to help men accomplish their all important task of shaping their children in such a way that they would impact their generation.

Francis Edo Olotu

FOREWORD

A considerable volume of literature is available in the areas of mothering and motherhood. Little, however, is found under the subject matter of fathering or fatherhood. It is in the light of this that Dr Francis Edo Olotu's *Releasing the Power in Fatherhood: The Dynamics of Effective Fathering* is found not only to be timely but tremendously relevant in the general exercise of parenting, especially in the context of the socio-political and economic realities of contemporary African situation. The book is not only an invaluable scompendium of ideas and facts, but also spirit-filled, strategic and well-targeted. It is a book that shows mastery of scholarly research and depth. A strong indication in the book is that fathers play indispensable role in the building of the home and society. Therefore, to become a good and influencing father, the qualities necessary for achieving effective fathering must be consciously cultivated. In its general understanding, parenting, and fathering in particular, is sometimes taken for granted, and so minds and hearts are usually not applied in a conscious manner to the exercise of fathering.

Dr Francis Edo Olotu's *Releasing the Power in Fatherhood: The Dynamics of Effective Fathering*, among other things identifies the place of naming at the very cradle in the life of a child, and connects the child's growth, personality building and general development to the child's social network and the place of the father in the scheme of things. The author ties the love that exists between husband and wife to the discipline of a child. He considers the father as a mentor for the child – a mentor born out of love, prayer, discipline and closeness to the child. Thus, the father plays the role of a teacher, a friend, a pastor, and a counsellor to the child's hope, vision and focus. Specifically, the author also examines the father's inputs on the child in the areas of skills acquisition such as speaking and listening, reading and writing, critical thinking, decision making, management, as well as choosing a career. In other words, the father is not just a medium of exposure for the child but more seriously a link between the child and the world of experience called LIFE.

It is pertinent to note that the general practice has been that the bringing up of children is best reserved in the act of mothering, or as part of motherhood. And so, fathers almost usually feel exempted from the day-to-day mentoring of the child. But for Dr Olotu, fathering is a call, a duty, an obligation and a challenge as it has to do with ushering into life children and giving them principles of living a fulfilling life. This book is a must-read for all who are involved in the very act of bringing forth and bringing up children.

Dr Isaac E. Ukpokolo,
Department of Philosophy,
University of Ibadan,
Ibadan

ABOUT THE AUTHOR

Dr Francis Edo Olotu is the Medical Director of Christ Hospital, Ondo, Ondo State, Nigeria. He has been in Medial Practice for thirty years after graduating from the College of Medicine of the University of Lagos in 1979. He is a member of the Nigerian Medical Association and the Association of General and Private Medical Practitioners of Nigeria.

He has had a burden to write on fathering after observing the deficits in the lives of men and women he had interacted with over the years whose travails in life are traceable to either father-absence or minimal father involvement in their upbringing. There is a dearth of books on this subject and his decision to write was prompted by this acute need to tell men what fathering is all about and how to go about it from cradle to adulthood. He had at various times served as a leader in the Catholic Charismatic Renewal of Nigeria, Full Gospel Businessmen's Fellowship International and the Association of General and Private Medical Practitioners of Nigeria. His serving in executive positions in all these bodies brought to the fore a need for books on the subject of Fatherhood andFathering.He speaks often on Marriage and Family in many tertiary institutions in Nigeria and this has opened his eyes to the needs of a young father who constructively wants to be involved in his children's lives. He is happily married to Bukie and they are blessed with four wonderful and well-adjusted children who love the Lord and are serving Him wholeheartedly.

He is the author of A Guide To Cancer Prevention and the Amazing Power in Fatherhood. Dr Olotu established Christ Hospital 20 years ago where he practices holistic medicine. He continues to speak and write on family and medicine-related issues.

INTRODUCTION

So little is expected from fathers in terms of input in the life of a child because Society believes albeit erroneously that the home belongs to the mother. The truth is, the father has as much stake as the mother in how his children turn out in life. A lot of fathers may not know how to constructively engage their children in ways that would develop and transform them in to successful children. This is because a father whose dad had little input in his life may not have much to offer his child. This book was written to address this need.

This book incorporates some topics in the University of Toronto Quality of Life Model which had identified through research factors that contribute to the goodness and meaning of life as well as people's happiness. Some of the skills also discussed in this book were adapted from the report of the committee set up by the United States Secretary of Labour in 1990 to identify the set of competences and foundation skills known as SCANS [Secretary's Commission on Achieving Necessary Skill] which everyone entering the work force needed to have. These topics are meant to thoroughly equip your child for the challenges of life.

My most compelling reasoning for writing this book was the positive feedback my wife and I got from our children of ages 22 and 19 in tertiary institutions of learning about the impact of home training on their lives. They believe the training they got made a difference in their lives and they hope to pass such on to their own children.

I have been a regular conference speaker in tertiary institutions on the subject of marriage and family for over two decades and from the feed backs I regularly get from these students, a book of this nature will help them in playing their fatherly role when the time comes. It is a hands-on training manual for a father who knows very little about fathering.

Having also served in various leadership roles in the Catholic Charismatic Renewal as well as the Medical Profession in Nigeria, I have seen first hand, the difference the skills discussed in this books makes in the lives of those who have them while those who lacked them were severely handicapped in the offices they occupied. A person has a better chance of succeeding in whatever position he finds himself when he is well equipped with these skills.

Many successful men and women across different walks of life link their success in life to what they got from home and many specifically mention their dads as their mentors. When men believe in anything, they have a way of giving it pride of place in their scheme of things; my desire is that this book will fall in to the hands of men who have accepted the fathering challenge and are willing to do all within their power to raise successful children.

My book will provide bonding between fathers and their children which is lacking in many father-child relationships. There are so many fathers and children that are emotionally distant from one another and it becomes painfully apparent that the opportunities for bonding were lost in the critical formative years of the child. New generation of fathers must learn from this and be involved in the lives of their children to the extent that through out life, a strong bond will exist between a father and his children. Any father who practices most of what is in this book will have his children as his best friends because his heart will be turned to them; in this way he will be fulfilling Malachi 4:6[The last verse of the Old Testament] which expressly commands fathers to be involved in the lives of their children.

The book is arranged in seven parts to cover the perceived needs of a child in the first twenty years of his life that would make him successful in life. My wife and I applied these facts in raising our children and we saw the difference they made in their lives; our children will readily attest to the validity of all I have stated in this book. Every chapter educates the reader on the subject of the theme before delving in to strategies on how to implement the ideas in the home setting. The section on life application helps the reader reflect on what he has read and how to personally incorporate these ideas in his relationship with his child.

There is a list of reference books, articles and web addresses which gives more in-depth coverage to the topics discussed in each chapter. Knowledge about child development is growing at phenomenal rate and no single book can exhaust all there is to know about this domain.

PART ONE:
FUNDAMENTALS OF FATHERING

"Life is no brief candle to me. It is a sort of splendid torch which I have got a hold of for the moment, and I want to make it burn as brightly as possible before handing it on to future generations".

George Bernard Shaw

"Someday you will know that a father is much happier in his children than in his own. I cannot explain it to you; it is a feeling in your body that spreads gladness through you."

Honore de Balzac

CHAPTER ONE

The Difference a Father's Love Makes

FOCUSING QUESTION?

1. *How would you describe a father's love?*
2. *In what tangible ways can a father express his love for his child?*

A FATHER'S LOVE

A father's love is that strong feeling of affection which a man has for his children that would make him protect, provide and nurture them while seeking their ultimate good in the process. It is a keen recognition that these children are your offspring and would depend on you for their physical, social and moral upbringing. It is an intense, deliberate and unconditional love which is measured by the extent to which a father is willing to make sacrifices for his children. A father's love is always intentional and dynamic; it cannot be hidden or glossed over when present in a man. Children who receive adequate doses of this love are self-confident and well prepared to seize the chances life offers them to make a successful living. A father who never experienced this love can nevertheless seek to give it to his children by reading about it and passing it on to them.

AN EXAMPLE OF A FATHER'S LOVE

When Ulysses S. Grant heard the news of his father's death while he was president of the United States, his grief was devastatingly deep. He owed so much of his success to his father who compelled him to attend West Point, a US military academy at the age of seventeen. Ulysses before this time lived an indolent life, having been brought up in opulence. He was only interested in riding horses and even the family business held no attraction for him. Even his mates found him boring, confused and aimless that they nicknamed him "useless". His father intuitively knew he was ill equipped for adult life and despite his protestations, used his influence to get him into West Point, the US Military Academy, where purpose and direction were given to him in just one term. "The harsh plebe summer, the rigid discipline, the spit and polish, the painstaking attention to detail of West Point" rescued the life of the man who went on to win the US civil war and become the President of the United States. His father, Jesse Root Grant, realized his mistakes in pampering him when at age seventeen he was of no use to anybody. It was a father's love that drove him to do the needful to save his son from the brink of the precipice.

Loving a child does not mean giving in to all his whims; to love him is to bring out the best in him, to teach him to love what is difficult"

Nardia Boulanger

30 Practical Ways of Showing Love to Your Children

You can do so in the following ways: **By preparing yourself to be a responsible father.** You have got to make up your mind to be a responsible father before marriage by reading books on fatherhood, attending seminars and developing yourself in your areas of need. You have to choose a spouse who shares similar vision and values with you about the family. You must be willing to transmit the good values put in you at home while growing up and at the same time leave off any "excess luggages" from your background.

From Conception to School Age

From conception till birth place your hands on your wife's abdomen regularly and bless the baby. Declare that your baby will be perfectly formed and will be beautiful to behold. Declare that your wife will have a trouble free antenatal and delivery experience. Praying for your unborn baby creates a bond between you and your unborn child. **Give your baby a meaningful name at birth.** The bible records the incident when God changed the name of Jacob to Israel while Jesus changed the name of Simon to Cephas. Jesus was named Emmanuel while yet unborn. Children have an uncanny way of living up to the meaning of the name they bear. **Dedicate your child to God at birth.** Do so on a regular basis while carrying your baby. The prayers of a father for his child are very potent. Jesus was presented to God in the temple according to the Jewish custom. Pray for your child using the words in Numbers 6:22-25 **Read to your child.** Children love the sound of your voice, read

portions of the bible and children's books. Reading to your child has been found to lead to optimal language development, good vocabulary development, and clarity of speech will make the child talk earlier than his/her mates. As from 3years of age, introduce nursery rhymes; this has been found to improve the child's reading skills. **Keep Health Records.** Visit your paediatrician or family doctor to find out if your child's immunizations are up-to-date. Make sure your child gets the necessary vaccinations against prevalent childhood diseases for which there are vaccines. **Provide Safe Day Care.** Visit your child's day care centre to be sure the setting is safe, hygienic and developmentally appropriate. Make sure sedatives are not given to the babies routinely to make them sleep so that the baby minders will have less work to do. **Provide safety at home.** Check your home periodically for possible dangers and remove them. Be sure medicines, cleaning supplies, sharp objects and other potential hazards are locked up and kept out of the child's reach. Be particularly careful with children that are 3years or younger who can choke with objects in their mouths. Protect your children from sexual molestation. **Provide safe transportation**. Infants and children younger than 12 should be put in the back seat of the car, not the front seat particularly if the car has an airbag. Be sure your child's safety seat is installed properly and make sure it is appropriate for the weight and height. Insist that your child buckles up just like you. **Make your child happy.** Give your child a hug, cuddle, pat or whatever gesture of affection your child loves especially when the child is unhappy. **Give appropriate diet.** Make sure your child is given nutritious diet from a tender age. Remember that the seed of obesity is sown in childhood. Watch your child's weight also and seek professional help if the need arises. **Be involved in nurturing and caring for your children.** Be involved with your children from the time they are born, bearing in mind that it is only breast feeding you cannot offer your child. Participate in caring for your children.

"A man never stands as tall as when he kneels to help a child"
Knights of Pythagoras

SCHOOL AGE TO TEENAGE YEARS

Affirm your child and demonstrate love without inhibition. Ann Landers received a letter from a mother asking her at what age a father and son should stop kissing and saying "I love you" to each other. Ann Landers gave the mother a one word answer: "Never". Shortly afterward Ann Landers received another letter from a father. He said her response to the mother's letter moved him to tears. He explained why: "A few weeks ago I kissed my son for the first time and told him I loved him. Unfortunately, he did not know it because he was dead. He had shot himself". The father continued: "The greatest regret of my life is that I kept my son at arm's length. I believed it was unmanly for males to show affection for one another I will never recover from this ignorance and stupidity"

1 Jn 3:18 'my children let us not love in word or in tongue, but in deed and in truth'.
Make fatherhood a priority Plan your work around your family with the mind set that father-child time is non negotiable, but work time is. Make the sacrifice that would enable you have contact always with your children as they are growing up. Children measure how much you love them by how much contact you have with them. Everyday contact is regarded by them as lots of love. When you have to be away, keep in touch with them by phone and emails as the case may be. Because children's greatest fear is being abandoned by you; you build a sense of worth in them when you listen and allay their fears when they feel lonely or threatened. Have a regular one-on-one time with each child; make it a period when you turn off the TV, computer, put down the newspaper and give your children undivided attention. **Lead your children to Christ** Lead your child to a saving knowledge of Christ and oversee his development of spiritual values. **Introduce discipline into the life of your child.** Let him know the operating rules and behaviour boundaries in the home. It prepares him for life because every action in life has its consequences. Let punishment be spelt out for every infraction of the rules in the house. **Introduce him to personal hygiene as he grows up** Let him learn to keep his clothes and room clean as well as learn to keep his person well groomed. **Maintain a happy relationship with your wife** Children feel loved and secure when you are visibly happy and demonstrate affection to your wife. In times of divorce, children feel guilty because they think they must have contributed to the marital strife. Mutual dependency grounded in the realities of gender complementarity which is the hallmark of happy marriage goes a long

way in making a child feel loved. When your relationship with your wife gets sour, with time, it spills over into the father-child relationship. **Gather fathering skills** Keep acquiring skills pertaining to child rearing from informal discussion with other great dads, attending parenting classes, reading books and articles, and listening to tapes on fathering. **Motivate your children with positive words.** Use phrases such as "You can do it", "You're such a terrific girl" liberally. It nurtures your child's self esteem and self confidence when you praise her efforts on doing anything good. **Connect with your child at all levels** Visit her school, meet her teachers, check her books, check on her co-curricular and extracurricular activities. When any child is participating in a sporting activity, be there to cheer him/her. **Monitor your child's activities** Make sure they have set time for their meals, homework and games. Limit the time spent on watching TV and on the Internet and censor what is been watched or the kind of music being listened to. **Be your child's Mentor** Work to instill moral values into him as he grows up showing him what kind of person he should be and how he is to live. Tell him your expectations of him **Educate your child about puberty** Teach what changes to expect and why they should not panic because every person experiences these changes. **Tell him about peer pressure** Inform him early enough that all the good morals he has learnt from home will be challenged by some friends who do not share a similar conviction. **Tell him about the importance of his choice of friends** Teach him what to look for in potential friends because bad company corrupts

good morals. **Speak to them about their future careers** Find out his interests and choice of career. See that his ability and interest match his career. Make the services of a guidance and counselor available to any child that needs. **Inform them about experiences they can do without** Alert them to the dangers of alcohol, smoking, pornography, premarital sex and teenage pregnancy and exam malpractices. These vices can scar their lives and leave them with regrets later in life.

YOUTH YEARS

Prepare your child for marriage

Teach them what personal preparations they have to make to make them eligible spouses. Teach your son what true masculinity is and role of a husband in marriage. Teach your daughter what to look for in a potential suitor and the role of a wife in marriage. Let her know that culinary and home-making skills are vital in marriage. **Teach them employment skills** Your children need employment skills to bridge the gap between what they were taught at school and what industry demands. You can have your children attend seminars that will equip them with these skills

IN A NUTSHELL

Your children need your love to grow and develop into responsible adults.

2 Effective fathering entails your life being interwoven with that of your children. You are irreplaceable in the life of your child because you have so much to offer them. Even the best boarding school cannot take

your place when it comes to shaping your children for a successful life.

LIFE APPLICATION

Evaluate your self on the basis of the different tasks you ought to be involved in as a father and score yourself. A score of 80 percent and above is satisfactory. A score below 50 per cent means you are depriving your child of what will make him grow up into a responsible adult. Strengthen your connection with your children by getting more involved in their lives.

FURTHER READING

Brott, A. A, & Ash, J (1995) The Expectant Father: Facts, Tips and Advice for Dads to be. New York: Abbeville Press

Shaipiro. J. (1993) The Measure of a Man: Becoming the Father you Wish Your Father had been. New York: Delacorte

Levine, J. A & Pittinsky, T (1997) Working Fathers: New Strategies for Balancing Work and Family. New York: Addison-Wesley

CHAPTER TWO
Training Your Child

FOCUSING QUESTIONS

1. *What does it take a father to train his child?*

2. *In what areas does a child need training?*

3. *How is the training carried out?*

4. *What challenges does a father face in training his child?*

5. *What are the benefits of training your child?*

6. *What are the consequences of not training your child?*

THE IMPERATIVE OF TRAINING YOUR CHILD

Every profession has a body of knowledge which students must acquire and attain proficiency in before being certified. There is also an associated code of ethics binding members of different professions which they must subscribe to in order to retain their practicing license. Training is what unlocks the potentials in your child and gives her the edge over her peers. In training your child, there is no special school where you go for acquisition of the requisite knowledge. Parents use what they saw their parents do or their life experiences in this regard, their culture, what they learnt from school and church, what they read in books and from marriage seminars to model the training they give their child.

"There is only one way to bring up a child in the way he should go, and that is to travel that way yourself"

Abraham Lincoln

WHAT DOES IT TAKE A FATHER TO TRAIN HIS CHILD?

Love A father requires love to train his child; it is this love that drives him to make the necessary sacrifice to see that he is well equipped to face the challenges of their time. A father's love should be unconditional and patterned after that of God for His son, Jesus. God the Father demonstrated this in Luke 3:22 when at the baptism of Jesus Christ before the commencement of His public ministry He said, "You are my beloved Son; in you I am well pleased". Love your child for who he is and not for what he can do. Let him know that behind your demands is a loving heart that means well towards him. **Conviction** A father must be convinced that his child needs training and he is in a unique position to lead the team that will shape the future of his child through training. The team includes his wife, older siblings that are well behaved, a school that teaches good morals and a church that has good children's programmes.

Commitment and Tenacity of Purpose

Training your child requires commitment, focus and tenacity of purpose. You must count the cost in terms of time, energy and other resources when you resolve to train your child. The commitment is born out of the belief that your child is unique and has a lot to offer the world when he/she matures into a successful adult. Gleon Doman, the director of the Institute for The Advancement of Human Potential said, "Every child born has, at the time of birth, a greater potential intelligence than Leonardo da Vinci ever used". **Quality Time** You need good quality time to spend with your children as they are growing up. Children learn more by watching than hearing you. When you do things with your children, it enables them develop decision making and problem solving skills. They imbibe social skills such as communication skills, interpersonal skills and self regulatory skills readily. **Resources** You need knowledge, wisdom and child you are blessed with. Do not be ashamed to seek help in parenting and marriage classes, seminars or counseling if the need arises.

TRAINING NEEDS OF YOUR CHILD

There have been many studies carried out to determine the factors that guarantee successful living. Prominent among these is the World Health Organization's Quality of Life model as well as the University of Toronto Quality of life Research Findings. The two studies found that people who enjoy optimal quality of life are those who have developed their whole person. Your child needs training in the following domains of life:

The Spiritual Keeping fit spiritually by developing faith in God, studying the bible, learning to pray, attending church and being involved in Christian fellowship activities, etc. **The Physical** Maintaining good physical well being entails knowing how to stay in good health, developing healthy eating habits, maintaining good physical grooming, engaging in exercises, etc

The Social Your child will need to know how to relate to others by developing strong interpersonal and communication skills.

The Psychological You will assist your child in building his/her self-esteem, self-concept, self-reliance, self-confidence, self-regulation and sense of responsibility.

The Economic This has to do with development of good money management skills.

Moral values They equip your child to make the right decisions in life when he/she is away from you.

Life skills such as leadership ability, entrepreneurial skills and time management skills that will help your child live productive and satisfying life.

Community service and involvement would help your child live in such a way as to affect society positively

Leisure activities that will help him/her reduce stress and stress-related diseases in life.

Good character formation

THE ACT OF TRAINING YOUR CHILD

The bible in Proverbs 22:6 says: "Train a child in the way he should go, and when he is old, he will not depart from it".

Basically, this entire book is on the act of training your child so that she can become a productive and responsible adult. What you do as training can be divided into:

Training your child in the way she should go. This entails walking the way so that she can see it, catch it and make it a lifestyle.

Training up a child in the way she should not go. This entails using everyday examples of condemnable practices to instruct your child. **Doing things with your child [Hands on training]** When you give your child undivided attention and engage in one on one discussion on issues that bother him/her, you are able to counsel the child. When you watch his/her favorite TV programs, you use opportunities offered by the show to impart moral lessons to the child.

Things you will make your child do Eating the right food not just what the child loves, tidying the play spot, ensuring he/she does his/her homework, maintaining good personal hygiene are things you get your child to do.

Doing things to your child You discipline your child when the need arises.

You observe your child You check his/her diction and attitudes to be sure they are right.

Things you will allow to happen to your child Children learn fast when you allow them to suffer the consequences of their actions. A child that runs foul of school rules should not be shielded from the stipulated punishment.

Create a Memory Bank in your child Let there be events in the lives of your child that he/she can recall to make him/her walk on the good path you have chosen for him/her.

"We cannot always build the future for our youth, but we can build our youth for the future".
Franklin D Roosevelt

CHALLENGES FATHERS FACE IN TRAINING THEIR CHILDREN

Fathers may face the following challenges in training their children: **Knowing what constitutes proper training** Fathers, who were from homes where their father trained them, take to training their children naturally. They simply pass on with some modifications what they got from home. Men who grew up in fatherless settings or single parent homes will have to find out what is normal to give to their children. They can get the needed information from books, churches, parenting or fathering classes.

Making time available Your children need your physical presence to imbibe what you have to offer. You might need to switch to a job that gives you more time but less money to enable you achieve your goal. A self-employed person is more in control of his time and can determine when to be at home to meet his children's needs. **Confronting issues in your life** You may have moral issues in your life that rob you of the moral high ground you need to train your children in a godly way. Be courageous to deal with such issues for the sake of your children. **Maintaining harmony with your wife.** Your wife is a valuable partner who can enable you achieve your fathering goals. Build a happy relationship with your wife and you will have a person who enforces your rules in the home while you are away. She also makes valuable input into the training when your relationship with her is okay. When there is disharmony in the home, your wife may work at cross purposes with you in bringing up your children.

Enabling Home Environment Let all parties work to create the right environment for your children to develop. An unknown author summed up the effect of the home environment on children in the following sentences:

If a child lives with criticism, he learns to condemn If a child lives with hostility, he learns to fight. If a child lives with ridicule, he learns to be shy If a child lives with shame, he learns to feel guilty If a child lives with tolerance, he learns to be patient If a child lives with encouragement, he learns confidence. If a child lives with praise, he learns to appreciate. If a child lives with fairness, he learns justice. If a child lives with security, he learns to have faith. If a child lives with approval, he learns to like himself. If a child lives with acceptance and friendship, he learns to find love in the world.

Use of Time Regulating the time spent on watching Television, surfing the net and sundry activities that do not add value to your child's life is a big challenge. Limit the hours spent on TV and the net and you will find her grades improving while regulating her behaviour will be easier.

Patience Impatience which can result in physical and verbal abuse must be dealt with. Tell yourself that you are doing the noblest task on earth if you are tempted to be impatient.

Unavailability of Resources Absence of fathering or parenting classes in your vicinity makes your task more challenging because when you need assistance or counseling, help is not readily available.

Few Role Models Ever decreasing number of youth role models leave you as the sole role model she has at some stage in her life.

Peer Influence Peer influence arising from school and the neighborhood can corrode the morals of your child. It keeps you at alert to nip any negative habits in the bud.

Poor Economy Economic hardship might make you want to keep a good paying job that deprives you of the needed time with your children. You need to prioritize issues here. **Over commitment** You may need to scale down your social commitments as well as church commitments to enable you achieve your fathering goals during your child's growing-up years. **Knowledge Update** You may need to read relevant books and attend marriage and parenting seminars to bridge the gap between what you know and what you need to attain your fathering goals.

Decadent Society An increasingly decadent society will always pose a threat by corroding the morals you have instilled into your children. You have to use every opportunity to talk about consequences of prevalent vices in the society so that they will always follow the instructions they got at home.

WHAT ARE THE BENEFITS OF TRAINING YOUR CHILD?

Sense of accomplishment You will feel satisfied that you have programmed him/her for successful living. You will not habour any sense of guilt as far as your fathering role is concerned if he fails to tow the path you showed him. **Peace, Happiness, Respect and Longevity** Society puts a premium on fathers who raised godly, responsible children. They honour you and hold you in high esteem. **Longevity** Well trained children will not threaten your life either directly by physical violence or through the stress and heartbreak that social miscreants bring to their parents.

Public good Well trained children will always advance the cause of mankind in their generation. They will be a blessing to their fellow man.

Role Models They will replenish the stock of role models young persons need to encourage them on the path of responsible living. **Productive living will be their portion** Because they will be about legitimate dealings all their lives; they will not spend time in jail atoning for their reckless living. **Safe guard for the next generation** Well trained children turn out to be responsible parents who in turn will raise responsible children of their own.

WHAT ARE THE CONSEQUENCES OF NOT TRAINING YOUR CHILD?

A life of mediocrity An untrained child in this highly competitive society would not be able to compete and take the chances life offers him/her. Training adds value to the life of a child and enables him/her to achieve competence in those domains of life necessary for successful living.

A life of crime This beckons to those who are unable to achieve self regulation that comes by training. A life of crime will lead to imprisonment at some stage in life. **Estrangement** The child feels the father is responsible for his woes for not imparting to him what was needed to succeed in life. There are children who have assaulted their parents on this count and threatened them with death.

Shame Society looks at the parents of delinquent children as failures who have offsprings that are a threat to law abiding citizens.

Irreparable loss to society Society will be deprived of the input of a person who might have served mankind with his/her talents if he/she was trained.

IN A NUTSHELL

1. You have all it takes to train your child if you choose to do it.

2. You have to develop the various domains in your child's life for him/her to enjoy optimum quality of life.

3. A broad range of activities are required in the development of your child. Harmony with your wife as well as an enabling home environment are critical to raising successful a child.

4. There are benefits to training your child as well as consequences for not training him/her. The benefits of raising your child properly would be passed from one generation to the next.

LIFE APPLICATION

1. Just as the journey of a thousand miles begins with a step, so does training your child begin with a strong resolve. Put a picture in your mind of what your child is capable of becoming when he/she is well groomed, this will serve as a stimulus for action.

2. If there are issues in your life that will send conflicting signals to your child about living a good life, be courageous to deal with the issues. No price is too costly to be paid for the sake of your child.

3. Be optimistic that your child will respond positively to training and would turn out well.

FURTHER READING

Cloud.H, Townsend .J.,: Raising Great Kids

CHAPTER THREE
Spending Good Time with Your Child

FOCUSING QUESTIONS

1. *Why is spending time with your child important?*
2. *What constraints do fathers have when it comes to spending time with their child?*
3. *What activities can you engage in with your child?*
4. *What are the benefits of spending time with your child?*

TIME SPENT WITH YOUR CHILD IS IMPORTANT

Your most important gift to him is your time; children measure how much you love them by the time you spend with them. Good quality time is time spent on an activity of value to you and your child; it is a time for focusing attention on your child with a view to knowing your child's thoughts and feelings as well as challenges. It provides opportunities for self revelation and bonding between father and child. Usually such an activity is mutually beneficial from the point of parent-child relationship. Talking a walk with your child on a regular basis can serve both as an exercise as well as a time for building intimacy. A father that is physically present in the home but emotionally uninvolved in the lives of his children can be described as available but inaccessible to the children; he is almost as good as a physically absent father. A father who is present and whose children can relate to emotionally at any time is both available and accessible; he represents the ideal. A father can be physically absent but is in touch with his children through phone calls, text messages and electronic mails. Such a father is accessible to his children because he uses communication to mitigate the effects of his physical absence. Doris Curan, a parent educator, says the cry of children today is "Love me for who I am, not what I do. Love me for being, caring and sharing, and erring; not winning, placing and showing". According to the National Fatherhood Initiative, the typical American working father spends just 12minutes a weekday in one- on- one conversation with his children. This means that by the time most children reach age six, they would have spent more time watching TV than they will spend during their entire lifetime talking to their father. Research has found that children whose fathers spend quality time with have higher self- esteem, higher educational achievement, a more secure gender identity and greater success in life. A woman's career success is greatly influenced positively by her father's presence and attention.

CONSTRAINTS SOME FATHERS HAVE IN SPENDING TIME WITH THEIR CHILDREN

Different men have different reasons for not spending as much time as they would have loved to spend with their children. The following reasons feature prominently among their excuses:

Preoccupation with work The struggle in climbing the corporate ladder, and providing for the financial needs of the family leave a lot of men with little or no time for their children.

Ignorance of what the time spent with one's child means Many fathers' thinking is on the false premise that all that matters in fathering is providing for the material needs of his children; nothing can be further from the truth. Rabbi Neil Kursham had this encounter "A young man told me of a conversation he had in hospital with his father just before he died. The father, a perpetually busy man, had not spent much time with his child and the son expressed his regret that they had not shared more time together. The father responded by reminding his son that he had worked long hours in order to put food on the table to feed the family. The son remained silent, but in his heart he was yearning to tell his father that he had never been as hungry for food as he had been for his father's presence".

Absence of a father that spent time with them Some fathers never had a father who spent time with them. For such men the aphorism, "You cannot give what you do not have" stands true. Such men can overcome this barrier and invest time in their children.

Fear that familiarity may breed contempt Some fathers feel spending time with their children will diminish the awe children ideally should have for their fathers. This is an old fashioned mind set that results in social isolation of the father as he gets old because he has not taken time to bond with his children.

Not knowing what to do with children Some fathers do not want to appear foolish because they do not know what to do with their children. Such fathers can start with some activities listed in this chapter, gradually they will "learn on the job".

When the home environment is inhospitable When there is strife between father and mother, the home situation is not often conducive for any meaningful father-child interaction; the father flees the home under any guise.

"My dear father, my dear friend, the best and wisest man I ever knew, who taught me many lessons and showed me many things as we went together along the country byways."

Sarah Orne Jewett

25 CREATIVE ACTIVITIES YOU CAN DO WITH YOUR CHILD

The following activities can bring you and your child together:

Share stories with him. Children love stories even when you repeat same stories again and again. It does not take much to learn how to tell stories even if it does not come naturally to you.

Read newspaper articles to her or ask her to read particular articles in a newspaper. Ask her views about the issue discussed in the article; in this way you are not only spending time with your child but also stimulating her interest in reading, learning and valuing information.

Plan and take a vacation together. Ensure that you have quality time together during the vacation. Let your itinerary be light enough to accommodate periods for discussion with him.

Eat together, make meal time fun. According to Dr James E. Van Horn; Professor of Rural Sociology, Pennsylvania State Cooperative Extension, "Most of the child's basic learning takes place in the many informal situations that occur daily in the life of the family. These informal occasions for learning include all the times the family members are together doing ordinary things such as getting dressed, taking baths, preparing to leave for kindergarten, eating and so forth"(Van Horn, 1993). Meal times are good times to teach table manners and ensure your child eats the right food.

Be involved with his homework. It enables you know his strength and weaknesses as well as your child's impression of his school. You get to know if your child has learning difficulties and if the school is meeting hiss educational needs. You get to know what transpires in the classroom from your child's report. **Create a family evening.** This should be a light hearted time for members of the family to share meals, jokes, and stories. She might ask about some of your experiences while growing up; it could be a time for you to talk about your family tree. You can encourage your children to render songs or poems composed by them. Let it be an atmosphere that encourages creativity amongst family members. **Gardening with your child** You can talk while gardening. You can tell her about the

benefits of keeping the environment clean or having a beautiful lawn.

Watch a movie or TV program that has a lot of moral lessons for everyone. Recently, I watched the film Prison Break with my children; I had so much to tell them about life from the film.

Cook and eat a meal together. Teach your son how to cook; it is a good life skill that will make him "good husband" material when the time comes.

Go for walks together. It provides opportunities to talk while extolling the benefits of exercise.

Model how to express your feelings. Teach your children how to disagree without being disagreeable persons; how to respect other people's views without feeling threatened. How to accept people who reject your opinion without feeling it is your person that has been rejected.

Visit your Child's School/ classroom. Meet his/her teachers, commend them for the work they are doing. Ask for their comments about your child and what you can do to enhance his or her performance.

If you are a non- custodial father, make regular phone calls or plan lunch dates. There is still so much you can do if you are divorced from the mother of your children.

Make visits to the Park and Museum. Going to amusement parks and museums will provide relaxation for the family. It sends the message to the children that life is not all work; there is room for relaxation too.

Create a family tree or talk about your culture. List the positive and negative things about your culture; discuss the effects of some cultural practices on the society.

Teach your teenage children how to clean the car, check the radiator, and level of engine oil in the car. This is a good chore for them in the morning, it helps to develop a sense of responsibility in your children; it is a valuable input from the children into the running of the home.

Teach your children how to resolve conflicts and model that behaviour. When there are differences of opinion as is bound to arise when relating with people of different background, your child must be taught the importance of listening to others and respecting their views.

Go with your children to the library; teach them how to use the library. Learning is a life-long process and he who is keen on it must know how to use the library. **Teach your children how to surf the net.** We are in the information age where every child is inundated with loads of information on the net as well as in the media. Teach your children about the good sites on the net as well as the off limit sites. **Discuss with your children, their academic goals for the new session.** Motivate them to greater success.

Meet your children's friends Chat with them and get to know their background. Later discuss with your children the kind of influence their friend may have on them.

Watch a live game (Football, basketball) with your children Listen to your children's comments about the game; share in their in their excitement about the game. **Ask** your children their career goals, and create opportunities for them to know more about their careers of interest. Take them to the setting where they would meet professionals of the careers of their choice. Provide books on different careers for their perusal.

Listen to your children's favourite music, ask what they like about the music Tell them the difference between good and bad music and why they should stick to good music always.

Ask your children one skill they would like you to teach them. It could be learning to play the piano if you are good at it or any other thing.

"The happiest moments of my life have been the few which I have passed at home in the bosom of my family."

Thomas Jefferson

BENEFITS OF SPENDING TIME WITH YOUR CHILDREN

You are able to help them build positive self-esteem by expressing how much you appreciate them. Words of encouragement have a way of making a child try new things without worrying excessively about failing in his/her effort. Your children know that even if they fail, they can learn from their mistakes and try again.

You get to know them as unique persons and respect them for who they are. You also know their areas of need and so work to help meet these needs.

They learn to communicate through observations and interaction with their parents. They learn to express their needs as well as learn to listen. You are able to teach and model good values to them.

You are able to mentor your sons and give them guidance. They learn to control their behaviour.

You are able to correct them at an impressionable period of their lives before they become set in their ways

You have opportunities to listen to them and know what is going on in their minds.

You are able to provide inspiration and motivation to better behaviour when an occasion calls for it

You are able to teach them some skills you have that they lack.

You are able to model what fatherhood is all about for your children from what they have seen in your interaction with them.

CONSEQUENCES OF NOT SPENDING TIME WITH YOUR CHILDREN

There may be no bonding between you and your children. You and your children will go through life as virtual strangers.

1. Your children are deprived of the valuable inputs you alone could have made into their lives. They enter life unsure of themselves and poorly equipped to compete in a tough world.

2. They could be exposed to crime at a tender age if you did not help them develop good personal value system.

3. They may pass unto their children their unfortunate experiences of "fatherlessness".

4. They too may not have time for you when you are aged and vulnerable. This excerpt from the Harry Chapin's "Cat's in the Cradle" says it all.

A child arrived the other day He came to the world in the usual way But there were planes to catch and bills to pay He learned to walk while I was away And he was talking' fore we knew it and as he grew. He said, "I'm gonna be like you, Dad

You know I'm gonna be like you". "When ya comin home dad? I don't know when But we'll get together then, yeah, We're gonna have a good time then…." I've long since retired, and my son moved away I called him up just the other day Said, "I'd like to see you if you don't mind" He said, "I'd love to, dad, if I could find the time. But the new job is a hassle and the kid's got the flu. But it's been sure nice talking to you". And as I hung up the phone it occurred to me. He'd grown up just like me. My boy was just like me

IN A NUTSHELL

There is no better way of showing your love for your children than spending time with them.

1. Time spent on your children is time well invested which will yield good dividends in the not too distant future.

2. There is a variety of activities you can engage in with your children depending on their ages.

LIFE APPLICATION

1. What new adjustments would you make to your schedule to enable you increase the number of activities you engage in with your children?

2. Remember no matter how busy you are, you can always make out time for what interests you or change your job as the case may demand.

3. The period it takes to climb the corporate ladder or gather wealth usually coincides with the growing period of your children and the time you are most capable of influencing them for good. Make the needed trade off now or else after you have gotten to the top of the ladder, your children would have left home poorly equipped for life.

FURTHER READING

Curran, D (1991). Delores Curran Talks with Parents. Family Information Services, Section 9, M & P 17-18

Harry Chapin, "Cat's in the Cradle", quoted in Edwin Louis Cole, Maximized Manhood: A Guide to Family Survival, Springdale Pennsylvania: Whitaker House, 1982 pp 58-59

Rabbi Neil Kursham, quoted in Mitch Golant and Susan Golant, Finding Time For Fathering; New York: Ballantine Books, 1992 p. 60

Chapter Four

Making Discipline a Learning Experience

Focusing Questions

1. What is discipline?
2.. What is the scriptural perspective on discipline?
3. Why is disciplining your children important?
4. In what areas do children need discipline most?
5. What are the guiding principles for disciplining a child?
6. What are the types of disciplinary measures you can apply to your children?

What Is Discipline?

Discipline is regulating the behaviour of a child to fit an acceptable norm. When you discipline a child, the message you are getting across is "what you have just done is inappropriate, and in future this kind of behaviour will not be acceptable". In this way, you make discipline an early life learning experience.

The goal of discipline is to create respect for parents and authority figures and this precedes a loving relationship with parents. Without respect for parents, children do not respect others. Children would only accept your values if they respect you.

Discipline helps in creating a structured environment for the child where there are boundaries for what is considered acceptable behaviour. It is in such an environment that the child's rights and that of others are respected. Children need boundaries to feel secure, the way railings make you feel secure while climbing a staircase. A father has the authority to do what is in the child's best interest without negotiating with the child.

This is because he is older, has passed the route earlier on in life and is concerned to see that his child turns out well. Accepting a father's authority which is one of the goals of discipline prepares a child for accepting the authority of God.

"There are two great injustices that can befall a child. One is to punish him for something he didn't do. The other is to let him get away with doing something he knows is wrong".

Robert Gardner

Scriptural Perspective on Discipline

The bible considers discipline as a critical need in the early life of a child if he is to turn out a responsible and God fearing adult. Bible is replete with examples of persons whose lives were blighted from indiscipline for example Samson and the Sons of Eli.

Samson defied his parent's warning in Judges 14: 3 when he told him;

"Is there no woman among the daughters of your brethren, or among all my people, that you must go and get a wife from the uncircumcised Philistines?"

The strongest man in history went to an early grave working as a slave with his eyes plucked out because he neither obeyed his parents nor had regard for the commandments of God.

The sons of Eli neither feared him nor had regard for God. They did not heed his warning about the gravity of their iniquity against God as recorded in 1 Samuel 2:25, "Nevertheless, they did not heed the voice of their father, because the Lord desired to kill them"

The following bible verses also reveal the position of the bible on the issue of discipline: 1Tim3:4, 5 "One who rules his own house well having his children in submission with all reverence (for if a man does not know how to rule his own house, how will he take care of the church of God"?

God demands that a precondition for being a church elder is that one must have disciplined children. Eph 6:1-4 "Children, obey your parents in the Lord for this is right. Honor your father and mother, which is the first commandment with promise: that it may be well with you that you may live long on the earth. And you fathers, do not provoke your children to wrath, but bring them up in the training and admonition of the Lord".

Fathers should bring their children to obey them without having the seed of rebellion sown in them. Heb 12:5-9, 11 'my son,

do not despise the chastening of the Lord; Nor be discouraged when you are rebuked by Him; for whom the Lord loves He chastens, and scourges every son whom He receives. If you endure chastening, God deals with you as with sons; for what son is there whom a father does not chasten? But if you are without chastening, of which all have become partakers, then you are illegitimate and not sons. **For we have had human fathers who corrected us and we paid them respect.** Shall we not much more readily be in subjection to the Father of spirits and live? For they indeed for a few days chastened us as seemed best to them, but He for our profit, that we may be partakers of His holiness. Now no chastening seems to be joyful for the present, but painful; nevertheless, afterward it yields the peaceable fruit of righteousness to those who have been trained by it'.

Discipline and love are made to go hand in hand while the fruit of discipline is respect for parents. In Proverbs 22:15, Proverbs 13:24, Proverbs 29:15, the bible supports the use of corporal punishment to effect discipline.

THE IMPORTANCE OF DISCIPLINE

Discipline that is done out of love has the following salutary effects on children:

Acceptance of the authority of Parents
Leadership of parents plays a very significant role in the development of a child. As primary care givers, they observe and mould their children with instructions and corrections; the evidence of accepting the authority of parents is in children keeping to the admonitions of parents. When a child submits to the authority of his/her parents, the child readily accepts

the authority of other significant persons who will later have influence in his/her life such as teacher, religious authorities, police, employers etc. Discipline is the foundation on which an effective parent-child relationship is built. **Provides security for the child** It enables the child know the boundaries of what is considered acceptable behaviour. Your child grows up confident knowing right from wrong when he/she is well disciplined.

Behaviour Regulation It teaches the child behaviour regulation which enables the child to behave properly at anytime and any where.

Keeps the child out of trouble A child that is used to observing rules will accept the rules of government and those in authority over him as a natural thing.

Produces peace and happiness in the child Discipline makes a child happy because there is no fear of impending punishment for violation of rules.

Makes a child stand out among his/her peers A disciplined child will always have opportunities to play leadership roles among his/her colleagues because he/she can be trusted to do what needs to be done. **Imparts Self-Management Skills** A disciplined child is able to manage his/her affairs in such a way that set goals are achieved. **Discipline will bring out and amplify the talents in a child** A disciplined child will keep the rules that will enable the talents in him/her to be recognized and put to good use.

Discipline will provide guidance Until a child matures to be on his/her own; discipline will enable him/her to follow the right path and after maturity will keep him/her on the good path.

"Discipline doesn't break a child's spirit half as often as the lack of it breaks a parent's heart."

Anonymous

ASPECTS OF LIFE WHERE CHILDREN NEED DISCIPLINE

1. Obedience to parents' instructions
2. Being honest
3. Not taking what belongs to others
4. Keeping to rules at home, school and church
5. Maintaining good behaviour at home and at school
6. Forming good habits
7. Personal cleanliness
8. Studying hard and doing homework/assignments
9. Time spent on watching TV
10. Respect for Parents and elders
11. Punctuality at all occasions
12. Truthfulness even at the risk of being punished for an offense
13. Respect for school and other constituted authorities
14. Returning toys after play/keeping play spot clean
15. Waking up early and laying beds
16. Civil diction and avoidance of swear/curse words
17. Doing household chores
18. Moral decency

GUIDING PRINCIPLES ON DISCIPLINING A CHILD

The following principles should be followed when disciplining your child:

Discipline out of love Because you have the best interest of your child at heart, you will not permit the child to be deprived of the avalanche of good that comes from discipline. Your child may not like it initially, but later he/she will show appreciation for it.

Define the boundaries of what you consider acceptable behaviour before enforcing it. The biblical aphorism that says "where there is no law, there is no sin" should be followed; do not punish children for offenses committed when there were rules in force. Come to the level of your child's understanding in spelling out acceptable behaviour and make sure it is enforced. **Always tell the child where she has erred** The child needs to know the basis for the punishment so that she will learn from the occasion. **Respond to defiance with decisiveness** Always nip the seed of rebellion in the bud. Defiance portends grave danger to the child and society and must not be overlooked. Children will from the earliest years want to know how strong or determined their parents are by putting up a show of contest of wills. A parent who backs out will be held in silent contempt by his/her child. Get the child to always do what you want him/her to do very early in life.

Distinguish between willful defiance and childish irresponsibility. Childish irresponsibility requires more understanding, explanation and correction regarding what is proper behaviour by the parents. Do not make impossible demands of your children; this will either discourage them or provoke them to wrath. Recognize the individuality of each child and stop trying to make one child a copy of the other. Demanding a high academic performance from a child with learning difficulties would lead to frustration in the child.

Reassure your child of your love at the end of a disciplinary measure. The goal is to let your child know that inspite of his failings, you still love him and would want him to turn out well in life. Demonstrate affection for your child by giving him a hug after disciplining him. Pray with him for grace to live by the lesson he has learned from the incident.

EFFECTING BEHAVIOURAL CHANGE IN PRESCHOOL CHILDREN

Children in this age group think principally about themselves only, however as they get older, they learn to think of others. You can greatly influence their behaviour by:

1. Helping them understand their feelings and the feelings of others.

2. Encouraging them to express their own needs to you while you try to meet these needs.

3. Assist your children in solving their own problems and give them opportunities to improve on themselves.

4. Praise them for observed good behaviour.

5. Tell them your expectations about their behaviour.

DIFFERENT TYPES OF DISCIPLINARY MEASURES

Disciplinary measures vary according to the age of the child, cultural values and the laws of the country. The following considerations must be borne in mind whatever the measures that are being taken:

Let your aim be to shape your child's will without breaking his spirit. You can break his spirit with words like "You have been a problem child since birth".

The interpretation you give to your child's behaviour is what determines whether the child needs discipline or not and the type of disciplinary measure he needs.

Types of disciplinary measures

Reprimand You scold a child verbally against future repetition of an unacceptable action. "I" messages are better in conveying messages of correction than "You" messages because they are less threatening. "You" messages are used to emphasize authority. This is an example of an "I" message, "I do not like you coming home late from school because it makes me fear for your safety". The "You" format of the same message is "You always come home late from school and this makes me fear for your safety".

Time out This is when you ask the offending child to sit or stand quietly in a corner to reflect on his/her bad behaviour. It is good for children over 18 months. It is advisable to use 1 minute for each year of a child to gauge the duration of time out. Next, make the child apologize for the inappropriate action. Hug the child and pray with child at the end of the incident.

The benefit of time out is that it helps the child connect action with consequences.

Logical Consequences This is when you allow a child face the consequences of his/her actions. A child who shoplifts should be made to return the stolen item to the shop owner with apologies for the misdemeanor. A child that did not take his/her studies seriously and ends up repeating the class learns to associate good academic performance with intense studying. **Withholding privileges** You can withhold privileges from a child that abused it or misbehaved.

Corporal punishment [Spanking] This is the most controversial of all the disciplinary measures. There are some countries where it is illegal to spank a child while some elites do not want their children spanked for any reason. No doubt, of all the disciplinary measures, this is the one most likely to be abused. Generally for very compliant children spanking is rarely required, but for disobedient children who require a painful stimulus stronger than the pleasure of a disobedient act, spanking becomes a measure of last resort. Family Research Council of America found that more than four out of five Americans who were actually spanked by their parents as children say that it was an effective form of discipline[2]. The following are some of the arguments against spanking from Den A Trumbull's seminal work:

1   It teaches a child aggressive behaviour. This is not true; rather it is the prudent use of disciplinary spanking that is an effective deterrent to aggressive behaviour in some children[3]. There is no evidence in medical literature till date that has linked a mild spank to

the buttocks of a disobedient child by a loving parent to aggressive behaviour in a child; rather childhood aggressiveness is closely linked to maternal permissiveness and negative criticisms of the child. It is the quality of parenting that determines how a child turns out[4].

2. Physical punishment is harmful to a child; the truth is, any disciplinary measure can be harmful to a child's emotions if carried to extremes.

3. It can create anger and resentment in a child. This is common to any disciplinary measure that is not corrective in purpose but vengeful and retributive in nature.

4. Physical punishment is an ineffective solution to misbehaviour. Several studies by child rearing experts have found that spanking a toddler in ideal situations is a powerful motivator to correct behaviour and an effective deterrent to disobedience[5].

5. All who were spanked as children are at risk of using violence to resolve conflicts when they are grown. The studies of Dr R.E. Larzelere [Director of research at Boys Town, Nebraska] and Dr Leonard Eron[University of Michigan's Institute for Social research] debunked this, they concluded and established that any association between spanking and antisocial aggressiveness in children is insignificant and artifactual[6].

6. Spanking gradually leads to physical abuse by parents who use it. This is untrue as spanking and physical abuses are two different entities; proper use of spanking may actually reduce a parent's risk of abusing the child. Swedish experiment to reduce child abuse by banning spanking is failing because in 1980, one year after the ban, rate of child beating was twice that of the US. Swedish report of child abuse by family members rose four-fold from 1984 to 1994, while reports of teen violence increased nearly six-fold[7]

WHEN DO YOU RESORT TO SPANKING?

In the following situations, after a child has received as much encouragement and praise for good behaviour as correction for bad behaviour:

1. Insulting the person of a parent or being disrespectful. Calling a parent name or saying "he is stupid" is an assault on the dignity and authority of the parent.

2. When a child deliberately and persistently defies a parent's instruction.

OBSERVE THE FOLLOWING WHEN A CHILD DESERVES SPANKING:

1. Spanking should be a planned action and not an impulsive reaction to misbehaviour.

2. Only a parent or authority figure should spank the child.

3. Spanking is more effective for those in 2 to 6 year age bracket and is rarely effective in those above 10 years of age.

4. Spanking should not cause injury to the child or leave a permanent scar.

SPANKING AND PHYSICAL ABUSE CONTRASTED

Spanking is application of one or two spanks to the bottom of a disobedient child while physical abuse is striking a child repeatedly and this may take the form of blows, kicks or punches to the child. While spanking is done out of love to correct an erring child, physical abuse is intended to hurt or injure a child. Spanking does not cause emotional hurts whereas physical abuse leaves injury marks on the body of the child. Physical abuse also damages the self-esteem of the child.

THE WAGES OF INDISCIPLINE

They include the following;

1. Brushes with authority and the law which may lead to prison sentences

2. Inability to attain set goals

3. Lost opportunities

4. Under performance

5. Condemnation to mediocrity

IN A NUTSHELL

1. Discipline is one of the responsibilities of parents that cannot be shirked without dire consequences to the child, family and society at large.

2. Children need discipline to survive in this world just as much as they need food, water and air to survive in this physical world.

3. A child without discipline may not achieve anything tangible in life because anything worthwhile has a price tag on it which only the disciplined can afford.

LIFE APPLICATION

Create a mental picture of how you want your children to turn out in life. Now, look at where they are presently and what they are contending with. What disciplinary measures do you think they need to achieve your vision for them? Do they need to play less and study more or do they need to be law abiding to obtain a good testimonial on leaving high school?

FURTHER READING

1. Novella J. Ruffin., Developing Responsibility and Self Management in Young Children: Goals of Positive Behaviour Management

2. Voter/Consumer Research Poll, National Values. Commissioned by the Family Research Council, 1994. 3.Den A. Trumbull; DuBose Ravenel: Spare the Rod? New Research Challenges Spanking Critics

4. [Olweus, Dan "Familial and Temperamental Determinants of Aggressive Behaviour in Adolescent Boys: A Causal Analysis". Developmental Psychology 1980; 16: 644-660]

5. Forehand, R. L. and McMahon, R.J. Helping the Noncompliant Child. 1981; pp.79-80 New York

6. Dr Leonard D. "Theories of Aggression: From Drives to Cognitions".Huesmann, L.R. [Ed] Aggressive Behaviour, Current Perspectives.1994; pp. 3-11, New York: Plenum Press.

7. Statistics Sweden. K R Info. May 1995; pp. 1-6

PART TWO: DEVELOPING SPIRITUAL VALUES IN YOUR CHILD

The father of the righteous shall greatly rejoice: and he that begetteth a wise child shall have joy of him"

Proverbs 23:24

CHAPTER FIVE
Your Relationship with God

FOCUSING QUESTIONS

1. *How does your relationship with God affect your children?*

2. *Why must you be both an example in godliness as well as a teacher of godly values?*

3. *How can you impact your children so that they will choose the path of godliness when they are on their own?*

4. *What challenges do ministers of the gospel have with raising godly children*

YOUR RELATIONSHIP WITH GOD IS IMPORTANT

Children cannot imagine or understand the person of God in the early years of childhood. You represent the clearest picture of who God is to them. If you are a warm and benevolent father that is the picture they would have of God. If on the other hand, you are a harsh and distant father, they believe God must be like their father.

Your relationship with God speaks a lot about your person and the person of God to your children. If you are serving God faithfully, your action is telling your children that God is good and worthy to be served. When you take time to let your children know why it is fitting and proper to serve God, they will begin to appreciate God to the extent of wanting to follow in your footsteps. A little child who watched his father take his wife and his children to church on Sundays, then went back home to read the newspapers asked his mother, "Mom when would I be grown enough to spend Sundays at home like daddy does instead of going to church"?

"Many of us have inherited great riches from our parents-the bank account of personal faith and family prayers."

Nels F.S. Ferre

YOU MUST NOT ONLY BE AN EXAMPLE BUT ALSO A TEACHER OF GODLINESS

The Bible has accounts of men who served God faithfully but their children did not follow in their footsteps. Every father has this concern of how his children will turn out in their relationship with God. The fact is, God has no grandchildren and the father-God relationship is not transferable; every child must seek God on his own.

Eli as a priest judged [ruled] Israel for forty years but in I Samuel 2: 12, it was written, "Now the sons of Eli were corrupt; they did not know the Lord". The prophet Samuel was another outstanding man of God whose children did not walk in his steps, in I Samuel 8:3, it is written, "But his sons did not walk in his ways; they turned aside after dishonest gain, took bribes and perverted justice".

You can learn from these instances by:

1. Explaining to your children in an age-appropriate diction, who God is and why you have chosen to serve him and live for him.

2. Explaining what it means to serve God to your children.

3. Explaining why some persons choose not to serve God or live for him.

4. Explaining and enumerating the advantages of serving God.

5. Explain and listing the disadvantages of not serving God.

6. Teaching them about the laws and moral attributes of God.

7. Using everyday circumstances that portray the advantages of serving God to speak to your children.

8. Use everyday circumstances that reveal the consequences of not serving God to speak to your children.

9. Let your children know about the challenges you face and how you tackle them; admit your failures when necessary to let them know how much you depend on the grace of God to live a godly life.

TEACH YOUR CHILDREN DILIGENTLY

God spoke to Moses in this regard in Deuteronomy in 6: 6-7

6 And these words which I command you today shall be in your heart;

7 You shall teach them diligently to your children, and shall talk of them when you sit in your house, when you walk by the way, when you lie down and when you rise up.

It is not enough to assume that because your children observe that you do not steal, they too would not steal. Explain to them in a language and manner they understand why stealing is condemnable. It is forbidden by God and by the laws of civil society. Tell them the advantages of not stealing and the consequences of stealing. Use everyday occurrences that highlight the subject of your teaching to rub in the message.

God expects you to use every occasion, not just family devotion times to teach your children about God and why godliness is a better option in life.

IMPACTING YOUR CHILDREN FOR GOD

The following measures will assist you in your goal to make your children serve God all the days of their lives:

1. Let your love for God be shown in your relationship with Him. Your set time of personal prayer, family devotion, church commitments and personal sacrifices for the kingdom of God communicate your love for God to your children.

2. Pray for your children daily and teach them how to pray.

3. Freely talk about your spiritual challenges to their hearing and measures you are taking to cope. Let them know the Christian life is not a bed of roses.

4. To some extent, try to mitigate the hardship your ministry brings on the family by striving to augment your income as well as meeting their material needs.

5. Let there be balance in your commitment to church and ministry.

Leave enough quality time to show love to your children by listening to them and meeting their needs.

6. Provide for their physical needs otherwise they will link godliness with being perpetually in need.

7. Correct, rebuke, reprove and train them in godliness.

8. Be an example in godliness. Do not use curse words on others.

9. Be faithful to your wife. Love your wife and show affection and deference to her in the presence of your children. She will enforce godly practices in the home while you are away.

   Make the home environment godly, let there be godly music etc. Listen to your children's music, find out what they like about it and find out if the lyrics are compatible with the upbringing you are giving them.

10. Ask them to invite their friends to your home. Interact with them to check if their morals will reinforce that of your children.

11. Find out what movies interest your children and if the movies will add value to their morals or corrode their morals. Advice them accordingly.

12. Introduce them to personal spiritual activities like having a quiet time and a time for personal bible study.

"We are to love God wholeheartedly and teach our children to do the same. That's the kind of legacy that will last

for generations and please God into eternity."
Bruce Bickel and Stan Jantz

MINISTRY AND YOUR FAMILY

Some ministers have wayward children similar to the cases of Eli the priest and Samuel the prophet. A minister's child, who was caught in the State of Florida with hard drugs, said he went into drugs as a way of venting his frustrations against God. He felt God took his father away from him because of his commitments as a minister that left him with little time for his family.

William Barclay, a leading Anglican Clergyman, scholar and author described the impact of ministry on the family in the following words

'As I look back on more than forty years of married life, I am astonished that the work of the ministry does not destroy ministers' marriages. The minister will have the best and biggest room in his house for his study. The minister sees less of his family than any member of his congregation does. He sees less of his children. He has to leave it to his wife to bring them up. Seldom can he have an evening out with his wife and, even when such an evening is arranged, something again and again comes to stop it. Demand to speak and to lecture take him constantly away from home and, when he does come home, he is so tired that he is the worst company in the world, and falls asleep in the chair. As I come near to the end of my days, the one thing that haunts me more than anything else is that I have been so unsatisfactory a husband and a father. As the Song of Solomon has it: "They made me keeper of the vineyards; but my own vineyard I have not kept". When the pastoral epistles are laying down the qualifications for the elder, the deacon and the bishop one of the unvarying demands is that "he must know how to manage his own household"- and for a minister that is the hardest thing in the world '.

To avoid the pitfall of Eli and Samuel, fathers who are into ministry should take the following measures:

1. Secure your home by being available and ministering to the needs of your children especially during the teenage years. Some children feel boxed in by "church" when their entire lives revolve round going to church services and other activities of the ministry.

2. Communicate with them on a one on one basis so that you can have first hand information on what they are going through.

3. Share your experiences with them so that they would not think you are using ministry to shy away from your family commitment.

4. Get the support of your wife to hold the forth or take up the slack caused by your ministry commitments. Respond promptly to distress call from her on any issue pertaining to the children.

5. Get your children to the stage of enjoying their walk with God rather than just having routine devotions to God.

6. Be involved in your children's lives.

7. Children are idealistic; when they see shortcomings in the lives of members of the church, they might reason that Christian standards are unattainable.

They can conclude that most church goers are hypocrites. You as a father while not exonerating any wrong doers should let them know about the propensity of man to sin; that is why we need to depend on God for grace to live as children of God.

8. Be willing to reduce your workload if your family commitments dictate so. The bible in 2 Tim 3:4-5 demands you're having godly children as a prerequisite for being and remaining minister.

IN A NUTSHELL

1. Your relationship with your children determines what impression your children would have of God.

2. Spiritual values are not only imbibed by children but should be taught by fathers.

3. You are in the best position to programme your children for godly living through activities which will make them experience the reality of God early in life.

LIFE APPLICATION

1. List some practical measures you would put in place to see that each of your children has a personal relationship with Christ.

2. In what ways can you adjust your programme to ensure that your children have more of your time?

FURTHER READING

William Barclay, Testament of Faith, Oxford: Mowbrays, 1977

CHAPTER SIX

Praying for Your Children and Teaching Them to Pray

FOCUSING QUESTIONS

1. *Why is it important to pray for your children?*

2. *Why is it necessary to teach them how to pray?*

3. *What are the prayer needs of your children?*

4. *How do I teach them to pray?*

5. *What are the challenges fathers face in playing this role?*

THE IMPORTANCE OF PRAYING FOR YOUR CHILDREN

Every Christian father has a responsibility of praying for his children, leading them to know Jesus as their personal Lord and Saviour and teaching them how to pray. The following happens when you pray for your child: **Guaranteed answers** There is a blood link between father and child that gives a father a legal right recognized in the realm of the spirit over his children. When he prays for his child sincerely, what he declares comes to pass. This could begin before the child is conceived; continue during pregnancy, birth and adulthood. Prayers during formative years are more significant and yield fruitful results.

You are fulfilling one of the expected roles of a parent. Your fatherhood is patterned after that of God the Father. The way God exists to bless His children, so you should be to your children. Their memory of you should be filled with your acts of benevolence and caring portrayed in praying for them. Praying for your children is a sacred duty which no father can claim exemption for.

It releases a father's blessing upon the lives of his children God has put a rich deposit of spiritual power in every father; those who are aware of this and tap into it are able to shape the lives of their children in very positive ways. Praying for your children is one of the priestly roles of every father. In praying, he offers his children to God and petitions God to protect, preserve and prosper his children. A father who prays for his children on a regular basis would grow in love for his children and be willing to make the necessary sacrifices to see that they succeed in life. A model of a father's prayer for his children as seen in Numbers 6:22-27 is worth following: **22 And the Lord spoke to Moses, saying: 23 Speak to Aaron and his sons saying, "This is the way, you shall bless the children of Israel". Say to them 24 "The Lord bless you and keep you: 25 The Lord make His face shine upon you, And be gracious to you: 26 The Lord lift up His countenance upon you and give you peace" 27 "So they shall put my name on the children of Israel and I will bless them". Your prayer has transforming power when it is laced with**

scripture. God in Isaiah 55:10-11 says **As the rain and the snow come down from heaven, and do not return to it without watering the earth, and making it bud and flourish, so that it yields seed for the sower and bread for the eater, so is My word that goes forth from My mouth: It will not return to me empty, but will accomplish what I desire and achieve the purpose for which I sent it.**

There is a great potential in every child to be an outstanding person in life; just as gold is mined in an impure form that makes it necessary to have it refined by fire to eliminate dross so that its purest form is obtained, so a child's mind can be beguiled by foolishness which robs him/her of all the talents he/she is endowed with. Your prayer would bring positive changes into the lives of your children.

Prayer makes your children amenable or responsive to godly wisdom as they grow up. Your children are growing up in a decadent world and are hearing so many discordant voices that aim to derail them from the right path. Your prayers have a stabilizing influence over their lives; they take to your advice readily because they know you have stakes in their lives.

You appreciate your children more Praying for your children increases their value to you and makes you ever grateful to God for them.

It makes you more fulfilled as a father As age takes its toll on your life, praying for your children easily becomes one of the things that will be indelible in the mind of your children.

Boosts the confidence of your children Your children go through life with confidence because they know their father prays for them. This is because they know they are not alone.

It leaves an example for them to follow and pass on to their children You become a role model for several generations to come because your children will feel the intervention of God in critical times in their lives and will share these with their children.

You become a watchman over your children A praying parent becomes more sensitive in the Spirit and more discerning when anything goes wrong with the child whom he prays for.

You discipline and correct them Because you pray for your children, you correct them when they err and they also accept your discipline and corrections because they believe it is for their own good.

Your children will reward you Children who are aware of the father's prayer input in to their lives are bound to bond with such a father and also appreciate such by caring for him in his old age.

"What other nation is so great as to have their gods near them the way the Lord our God is near us whenever we pray to him"?
Deuteronomy 4:7

PRAYER NEEDS OF YOUR CHILDREN

The prayer needs of your children are what you desire for your children and which you commit to God in prayer.

Spiritual needs: Pray that they would have an experiential knowledge of God very early in life the way Joseph, Samuel,

David, Daniel, Ruth and Mary knew God very early in life.

A Pray that God will fill them with a spirit of wisdom and revelation in the knowledge of Him. [Eph 1:17]

B Pray that the fear of God will be deeply entrenched in their lives.

C Pray that divine favour will be their portion in life.

Material Needs:

A Ask the Lord to protect them from every evil.

B Ask the Lord to put a spirit of excellence in them.

C Ask the Lord to protect them against the social maladies of this age.

Marital Issues: Pray for them to have the discerning heart to recognize the partner that suits them and the courage to wait till they encounter the right partner.

TEACHING YOUR CHILD TO PRAY

If the disciples of Jesus who were adults asked Jesus for lessons on how to pray, it is certainly in order for fathers to see it as an important responsibility to teach their children how to pray. Certainly what a father would teach depends on the age of the child.

From preschool to school age Teach your child how to pray by recitation. Use the word "talking to God" instead of "prayer" so that your child can relate to God as a person. Examples of such prayers are: As Morning Prayer: "Father, thank you for watching over me during the night, make me a good child, in Jesus name, Amen".

As Night prayer: "Father, thank you for all you did for me today, grant me a sweet night rest, in Jesus name, Amen".

1. Make them pray aloud so that they can hear themselves and be sure what they are saying makes sense.

2. Making praying a daily habit for them. You gain proficiency in praying by praying.

3. Saying of grace before and after meals increases their opportunities to pray.

School age upwards Your children in this phase of life can participate actively in family devotions by playing specific roles such as taking some intercessory prayer points. At this age, it is good to incorporate scripture parts into the body of their prayers. Examples of such scripture prayers are: The Lord will give his angels charge over me, so no evil shall befall me-Ps 91:11 The eternal God is my refuge and underneath me are His everlasting arms Deut 33:27 The Lord is my shepherd, there is nothing I shall want-Ps 23:1 **Faith Declaration or Confession.** This is a prayer that is loaded with scripture verses that address specific needs in the life of your child. The prayer is promised on scripture verses that say you can have what you say if you believe it-Check the following bible verses Mark 11:22-24, 2Cor 4:13, Proverbs 18:21 and Job 22: 28 **Here is a sample of such prayers I composed for my daughters**

I ----- [name of child] am an uncommonly beautiful daughter of the most high God. Jesus Christ lives in me and controls my life as my Lord and Saviour. The Holy Spirit is my teacher and he keeps me at peace. I love righteousness but hate wickedness therefore God has preserved me from all the evils of this age. I obey, love and cherish the word of God as well as the instructions of my parents and because of this the anointing of God is upon my life. I trust in the Lord with all my heart, I do not lean upon my understanding, in all my ways I acknowledge the Lord and so he directs my path. Academic excellence is my heritage in the Lord; therefore the Lord has made me head and not tail among my peers. The Lord has surrounded me with favours the way the mountains surround Jerusalem. At the right time, the Lord will provide me the bone of my bones and the flesh of my flesh as my life partner. I shall continue to wax stronger daily in the love, knowledge and fear of the Lord. God's angels continually encamp around me to deliver me from all evil. Thank you Lord for being my all in all, Amen.

My children recite these prayers to the hearing of everybody after the morning prayers while at home and on their own when they are not at home after their morning prayers.

CHALLENGES OF PRAYING FOR YOUR CHILDREN

A father may feel the response of his children to his prayers is rather slow and may be tempted to quit. This may be so with those who started praying for their children after they had grown and are hardened in their ways. Such fathers should note that prayers release power that keeps working in the lives of one's children long after death has silenced the lips of the father. Encourage yourself that you are doing the right thing and that your prayers will never be in vain. A praying father would of necessity live a more accountable spiritual life so that his

children would truly believe he is sincere in his concern for them.

"In all things count on God who does not change"
Hope Clarke

IN A NUTSHELL

A   Praying for your children is a sacred duty imposed on you by God. While it brings blessings on your children, it fills you with a sense of fulfillment and accomplishment later in life. It is never too late to start praying for your children.

B   Teaching your children to pray prepares them for a life of faith in God. It is never too early in life to experience the person of God.

C   Answers to your prayers for your children may take a while to manifest, do not grow weary and give up.

LIFE APPLICATION

Make a list of the prayer needs of your children; ask those who are of age what they wish you to pray about

Have a one-on-one discussion with each of your children about their prayer lives. Encourage them to pray even when they do not feel like praying.

FURTHER READING

Stormie Omartian; The Power of a Praying Parent.

CHAPTER SEVEN
Building Faith in Your Child

FOCUSING QUESTIONS

1. *How important is faith to your child?*
2. *In what ways can you model faith to your child?*

THE IMPORTANCE OF FAITH TO YOUR CHILD

It is often said that God has no grandchildren; your faith though personal cannot be transferred to your child. Every child must come to know, love and serve God by growing in faith. Every child was born with a measure of faith which must be nurtured. Faith can be defined as a strong belief in God that makes a child love God and want to keep his commandments and commit his/her live to Him. Joseph, Samuel, David and Daniel are youths who had strong faith in God as youths and can readily stand as models for young persons. Joseph, sold into slavery in Egypt would not yield to the solicitations of Potiphar's wife; rather he would ask rhetorically,

"How then can I do this great wickedness, and sin against God" [Gen 39:9]? Samuel lived with Eli who failed as a father in raising his sons to honour God; **1Sam 3:19 says "So Samuel grew and the Lord was with him and let none of his words fall to the ground".**

His mother's dedicating him to God at an early age and making regular annual trips to the Temple to worship God must have impacted him greatly. Daniel though exiled to Babylon and in the King's court

"Purposed in his heart that he would not defile himself with the portion of the king's delicacies, nor with the wine which he drank" [Dan 1:9]. David convinced Saul that he can defeat Goliath when he said **"The Lord who delivered me from the paws of the lion and the paws of the bear, He will deliver me from the hand of this Philistine".** They all earned their places in the pantheon of God's generals of faith.

"But without faith it is impossible to please God, for he who comes to Him must believe that He is, and that He is a rewarder of those who diligently seek Him."

Hebrews 11:6

21 WAYS BY WHICH YOU CAN MODEL FAITH TO YOUR CHILD

There are children who take to their father's faith readily and see it as the natural thing to do; some children are more circumspect and would want to see if there are better alternatives to following God. If a father takes the following measures, he will likely get his children to toe his line:

Who you are and your relationship with Christ

Passionately commit yourself to Christ and let the fruit of knowing Christ be evident to your child. The nature of your person has a lot to do with your child's faith in God. If you model the attributes of God such as love, compassion, mercy and kindness to him, he will take to God without much prodding. Teaching your child to have faith in God becomes more effective when he knows that your fatherly role and commitment to his progress in life is unshakeable. Children's perception of God emanates from who God is to their parents.

The Child-Father Relationship A child's relationship with the father goes a long way in determining her perception of God. A father that is distant and unloving makes it hard for his child to see God as a loving father since a child's image of God derives from what she knows about her father. When a loving bond exists between a father and his child, it becomes easier desiring to have the faith of the father and to model her father's spiritual life. A child that has been wounded by her father would find it hard to expect anything different from God. Have a loving relationship with your child and she would develop great faith in God. A good father-child relationship would always model a God-child relationship in a clear, positive and easy way.

Prioritize your family Let everyone know that next to the kingdom of God is your family. Some people's career had consumed their family because they did not have time to build their family. Deliberately make out time for each of your children and let that time be regarded as an important appointment that must be kept.

A Spiritually empowering Home Environment The atmosphere in the home affects the faith of children. Teach your family about God; do not assume they can read in-between lines from your relationship with God. Make talking about faith through testimonies of what God is doing in the lives of family members very natural in your home. In Deuteronomy 4:9 Moses said **"Only take heed to yourself, and diligently keep yourself, lest you forget the things your eyes have seen, and lest they depart from your heart all the days of your life. And teach them to your children and grandchildren"**. The goal is; **"That they may learn to fear me all the days they live on the earth, and that they may teach their children [Deut 4:10]"**.

Live out the Christian life in your home and admit your faults readily and let your children see your efforts at Christian growth. This will make faith both attractive and attainable.

Lead each child to a personal relationship with Christ It is important that each child knows the Lord Jesus as his/her personal Saviour. Let him/her know the implication of the decision to follow Christ. Help your children nurture their relationship with Christ. Create parent-child time in which the Bible is read and shared with the family.

The Family Altar A home where there is regular morning and evening prayers at set times in a particular place in the home gives God a special place in the home. The message the children get is that God is important and must be reverenced.

Church life A family who is actively involved in the activities of their church also tells the children that God is special and deserves our time and commitment.

Love your wife and keep your relationship aglow Children are most disposed to believe the bible as true and practicable when you love your wife because you are obeying Ephesians 5:19 which says

"Husbands, love your wives, just as Christ also loved the church". Loving your wife also banishes the fear of being abandoned by either of the parents which is a common preoccupation in the minds of children. Loving your wife puts your children's hearts at ease and makes them receptive to teachings on faith from either parent.

Put a premium on reading and understanding the word of God In the parable of the sower [Matthew 13:1-23], understanding the message is what differentiates those who bore fruits from those who lost their faith. There is a world of difference between factual knowledge and understanding what the issue is all about. Take pains and use everyday examples to make your children understand basic Christian themes like love, forgiveness and teach them how to apply such knowledge to daily living. Unless what you teach has some relevance to what the child encounters in real life, it may not have the desired impact on the child; he/she may forget it.**Real life experiences build faith** An ounce of real life experience has more impact than a ton of theological sophistries to a child. When God answers a family

prayer request, give praise and glory to God and call the attention of your children to it. An answer to prayer is a proof that God listens to our request and also answers them. Personal testimonies heard from the parents' lips portray God as God and as such, the child considers having a similar relationship with God.

Help your children develop a vision for God; help them discern the will of God for their lives Tell them about the purpose driven life. Jesus at the age of 12 asked his parents, **"Must I not be about my father's business "[Luke 2:49].**

Tell them your expectations of them; tell them you believe they will impact their generation for God. Tell them you believe they have all it takes to make a difference in the lives of different persons who will come their way. No matter their career in life, they should bring their Christian calling to bear on their jobs; they have been made ambassadors for Christ.

Acting out Christian themes When as a family you choose to provide financial support to an indigent student who is not related to you and you have no intention of making the person pay back your expenses on him or her; you are modeling unconditional love to your children. When you now teach about divine love to your children, they will understand it.

Remind them of their heritage If you have a family history of men and women who led consistent Christian lives; use it in highlighting the difference Christ makes in the life of individuals. Tell them to aspire to leave such a legacy of knowledge of Christ for generations unborn. Paul in 2Tim1:5 said,

"When I call to remembrance the genuine faith that is in you, which dwelt first in your grandmother Lois and your mother Eunice, and I am persuaded in you also."

Situational teaching Sometime in the recent past, a prominent Nigerian lost political office for claiming to have attended a University he did not attend. The man qualified for the office without resorting to lies; he resorted to lies because he wanted to be who he wasn't. I used the incident to teach my children about the consequences of telling lies. For persons who tell lies often, it becomes a habit; one day the truth will be known to the embarrassment of the liar. Every day life events will continue to demonstrate the superiority of godly living over ungodly living; fathers must not miss the opportunity to teach with such events.

Creating long term memories of faith-filled events When you want your children to remember one attribute of God, teach on the subject repeatedly and use recent events to rub the message in. Children have a lot of distractions to contend with, therefore work with this in mind and systematically remind them of what you want them to commit to long term memory.

Make learning about God fun Be creative in using hilarious situations to teach about faith. Jonah's experience in the belly of fish is one such example; it has humour and a message of how God can have his way in a person's life.

Do not discipline your children out of anger. Some of your bad traits while you were growing up will show up in your children; learn to manage your anger while trying to correct your children. Know for sure that you can never beat out of your children what is wrong in your life. A father that is mean, cruel, judgmental or difficult to please will make his children view God as a harsh taskmaster who is just waiting for opportunities to punish them. Explain to your children the rewards of children obeying their parents; it brings honour to their parents and blessings upon themselves.

3John4 says "I have no greater joy than to hear that my children walk in truth". Some of your children would be more challenging to raise than others; do not give up on them, rise up to the challenge depending on God's grace.

Participation in soul winning This would be a positive counter peer-pressure move that would make them have an experience of sharing the gospel with their mates early in life. Teach your children how to bear witness and lead others to Christ.

Teach them about the rewards of living a life of obedience to God The Rechabites can be regarded as the poster children of obedience. For generations, they kept to the instructions of their ancestors who forbade them to take strong drinks. When God asked Jeremiah to offer them drink in Jeremiah 35:6, they responded, **"We will drink no wine, for Jonadab, the son of Rechab, our father, commanded us, saying, you shall drink no wine, you nor your sons, forever".** Because of their act of obedience, God promised them, **"Jonadab the son of Rechab shall not lack a man to stand before me forever".**

"So then faith comes by hearing, and hearing by the word of God."

Romans 10:17

Provide age-appropriate faith building materials. Make books, stickers, comics, bibles and devotionals available in your homes and teach your children how to use them. Make them listen to Christian music and music that will not compromise their beliefs. Incorporating faith issues into a child's life all through his day to day activities is better done by people he relates with daily.

Positive peer relationships The bible says "Iron sharpens iron" and "Bad company corrupts good morals". Tell your children that they should be close friends with only those who share similar beliefs in God and have good moral values. They should be friends with persons who will reinforce the good values they believe in.

IN A NUTSHELL

1. The seed of faith is sown at home while your child is young; your role is critical in achieving this goal.

2. There are so many activities within your ability that can be initiated to develop faith in your child. A time given to such activities promises to yield good dividends

LIFE APPLICATION

1. Take out time and on a one-on-one basis ask your children what they understand about core Christian issues like baptism, conversion, the divinity of Christ, etc

2. Find out from them in what ways you can be an encouragement to them on matters of faith.

3. Find out aspects of Christianity that they find difficult to believe or understand. Encourage them to be frank and let them know your purpose of asking them is to clarify issues for them.

4. Ask them if they are finding their Christian faith exciting. What makes it exciting or unexciting?

FURTHER READING

Dr Earl R. Henslin, Man to Man, Nashville: Thomas Nelson Publishers, 1993

CHAPTER EIGHT

Wisdom Is an Asset; Help Your Child Get It

FOCUSING QUESTIONS

1 *What is wisdom?*

2 *Why is wisdom important?*

3 *What are some common misconceptions that children have that requires wisdom to correct?.*

4 *What is a father's role in making his children get wisdom?*

WHAT IS WISDOM?

Wikipedia defines wisdom as knowledge, understanding, experience along with a capacity to apply these qualities well in finding solutions to problems. It is the judicious and purposeful application of knowledge that is valued in society. You need wisdom to coordinate knowledge and experience to improve your well being. Nicholas Maxwell defined wisdom as the capacity to realize what is of value in life for one's self and others.

THE IMPORTANCE OF WISDOM

The bible unequivocally declares in **Proverbs 4:7 "Wisdom is the principal thing; therefore get wisdom, and in all your getting, get understanding"**. It also says in **Proverbs 8:11 that "Wisdom is better than rubies, and all the things one may desire cannot be compared with her"**.

Wisdom is the ability to apply knowledge in a way that is beneficial to the person; while it can be an acquired trait that comes from knowledge, learning, experience and understanding, it can also be divinely imparted as the case was with King Solomon. It enables you to deal wisely in your affairs. Wisdom adds value to your person and would make people want to learn from you.

"Don't be discouraged if your children reject your advice. Years later, they will offer it to their own offspring."

Unknown

WHY DOES YOUR CHILD NEED WISDOM?

The world is filled with so many discordant voices about what is good and bad; it takes wisdom to know what is right and keep to it.

Your child needs wisdom to enable him navigate the moral and ethical chaos that typifies modern day existence. Wisdom will improve the well being of children in the following ways:

Ability to provide answer to problems Wisdom provides necessary problem solving skills for your child to cope with the problems of life.

Self-knowledge Self knowledge enables a child to know his/her strengths and weaknesses, likes and dislikes and what to do in life **Understanding others** Wisdom gives you the uncanny ability to understand others and get along with them. This will boost your child's self confidence.

A good judge Wisdom will make you a good arbitrator in matters of dispute. As a judicial officer, you will be a wise judge.

A good leader Persons endowed with wisdom make good leaders because leadership is about making decisions and leading people on the right path.

Popularity People seek out people with wisdom for counsel. The Queen of Sheba traveled to seek audience with King Solomon when she heard of his wisdom.

Walking on the right path of life It takes wisdom to discover the right path in life and to walk on it. The bible talks of the path that seems right to a person but the end of it is death.

Balance Wisdom brings balance to a person's life.

COMMON MISCONCEPTIONS OF YOUTH THAT REQUIRE WISDOM TO CORRECT

Immature moral development and egocentric thinking describe the lifestyle of many youths; their thinking pattern is reflected in the following statements:

1. There is a short cut to success other than toiling hard.

2. You can afford to enjoy the pleasures of this world and defer serving God till you are 40 years of age.

3. If you are a big or powerful person, whatever you say or do must be the right thing.

4. If you were not caught doing the wrong thing, your action was probably okay. It is only wrong when you are punished.

5. You should ask "What is in it for me" before you render any service.

6. Your main reason for not cheating during an examination is because you may get caught, not that cheating is wrong.

7. Membership of cults projects your person and increases your popularity among your peers.

8. You can have unprotected sex and not get HIV infection.

9. The only way you can succeed in life is to go overseas where literally "money flows in the gutters".

10. Why work hard when you can get money through internet fraud?

11. Whatever the majority of your peers are doing at any point in time must be the right thing.

SOURCES OF WISDOM

No child is born wise; wisdom is an acquired trait and comes from the followings sources:

Divine Solomon prayed for wisdom when he ascended the throne of Israel and God granted him his wish. James 1:5 says if any one lacks wisdom let him ask God who gives wisdom liberally.

The Bible This has been a veritable source of wisdom for those who read it. It is the most widely read book in the world and has been a guide for those who are serving God on how to walk uprightly.

Words of our elders are words of wisdom Elders are supposed to be repositories of wisdom which they make available to their children. Most times children ignore such wise advice to their ruin.

Modeling wise actions or behaviour It's alright to copy or imitate an action that you have seen work. If you have a friend who lives within his means rather than on credit most of the time, he is certainly worth copying. There is no copyright control over his style of living.

Parents Parents by virtue of their ages and experiences in life have a lot to offer their children.

Wise sayings and anecdotes These are wisdom-filled sayings which children can imbibe into their lives to make them wise. Examples are: "A stitch in time saves nine" which means acting promptly will salvage a situation.

Knowledge Wisdom is the correct application of knowledge.

Experience The aphorism that "experience is the best teacher" is applicable in many spheres of life.

From Others You can also learn wisdom from the bitter experiences of others.

Intuition This is a kind of immediate knowledge of knowing what to do without the conscious use of your reasoning faculties.

14 SPHERES OF LIFE WHERE CHILDREN NEED WISDOM AND YOUR INPUT AS A FATHER

Seeking and knowing God early in life When you know God early in life, you avoid those pitfalls that lead to destruction or permanent scars in a person's life. Knowing God later in life is still better than not knowing him at all; however a person might have to live with the consequences of errors made earlier in life. It's been said that "though you cannot unscramble an egg", it can be turned into an omelet. Early knowledge of God delivers a youth from a scrambled life; it is one of the greatest legacies you can bequeath to your child.

Obedience to the word of God and instructions of parents It is wisdom of the highest order to use the Bible as a guide to know what is right from what is wrong rather than depending on the popular prevailing belief. Most parents believe it is in their best interest that you succeed in life and so their words of advice are packed with wisdom that would enable you achieve your goals in life.

Character Persons of good character are always in high demand and in short supply. Character communicates loudly and determines the greatness of a person. It is wisdom to let your child pay good attention to what it takes to build a good character. Attributes like integrity, temperance, fidelity, honesty, courage, justice, equity, fairness, patience, industry, simplicity and modesty define a good character.

Put a high premium on learning and education Aristotle said, "Educated men are as superior to the uneducated as the living to the dead". Education brings mental culture and opens doors which the uneducated cannot access.

Having a vision of whom and what you want to become in life. Every man is the architect of his own fortune. Great life is a summation or outcome of wise decisions made all through life. Just as a nation without a vision perishes, so a person without a vision would be stranded in life.

Friends and the company you keep Your friends are either a positive or a negative influence over you. Choose friends that will reinforce the good values you are nurturing in life. Friends who share identical goals with you will be a support to you in achieving your goals in life.

Management and use of time Time waits for nobody; time lost can hardly be regained. William Shakespeare in Julius Caesar said "There is a tide in the affairs of men which when taken leads to fortune; omitted, all the voyages of life is bound in shallows and miseries". Opportunities will always come, the issue is will you recognize them and seize them immediately?

Money management skills Wise use of money will deliver you from the debt trap that has caught so many promising persons. Living within your means and not trying to keep up with the "Joneses" will save you a lot of stress in life. The ability to save money for the rainy day will deliver you from financial distress.

Importance of life skills The world is full of social pressures that can either make you or mar you. Your child needs to be self-assured that he/she is competent and capable of working, able to situate himself/herself in the social world and is also able to develop and maintain close relationships with his/her peers.

The importance of good health Awareness of the importance of good health is best created as children are growing up. What constitutes good nutrition should be taught to children. The danger of over nutrition which manifests as obesity should also be taught to children. The place of exercise in maintaining good health should be stressed and children should be made to participate in exercises.

Recreation and leisure activities Stress is part of the realities of life as a person grows up. Inability in handling stress is one of the root causes of mental illness in today's world. Knowing what activities produce relaxation in you and indulging in them as often as is feasible is wisdom.

Who to marry There are spinsters and bachelors all around, yet it is only one person among the lot that you can choose as a spouse. It requires self-knowledge to know the attributes of who you wish to be your spouse and painstakingly find that person. You need wisdom to pick the right person to spend the rest of your life with.

What career to follow You need wisdom to match your interests with your ability in choosing which career to pursue in life. When you make a career choice, you have less stress and more pleasure on the job. Your creative abilities will be at their best.

Destroyers of youth Beware of smoking, alcohol, gambling, pornography, premarital sex, teen pregnancy, drugs and criminal activities that are prevalent in today's world. So many young persons have had their lives terminated or scarred by these vices. It is wisdom to shun these vices and walk uprightly. Remember that whatsoever a person sows is what it reaps; every action has its consequences.

"Nobody knows what a boy is worth, And the world must wait and see; For every man in an honoured place Is a boy that used to be."

Phillips Brooks

IN A NUTSHELL

1.Your child needs wisdom desperately to cope and make the right choices in life. You, as a father can help him/her get wisdom needed to succeed in life. There are many spheres in your child's life where he needs your wisdom to cope; avail him of your experience and words of wisdom.

LIFE APPLICATION

1. On a one-on –one basis, ask your children who their closest friends are and why they chose them. This will give you an insight into how they choose their friends.

2. Ask them one lesson they have learned in life they would not want to forget quickly.

3. Ask each of your children about the vision of who they want to be when they are fully grown. Ask them how they hope to achieve their dreams.

FURTHER READING

Proverbs chapter 8

PART THREE:
EARLY CHILDHOOD LEARNING

"Do not confine your children to your own learning, for they were born in another time."

Hebrew Proverb

"To be in your children's memories tomorrow, You have to be in their lives today."

Unknown

Chapter Nine

Recent Advances in Early Childhood Learning

Focusing Questions

1. *What is the new orientation in childhood learning?*

2. *When does learning start in a child?*

3. *How do Children Learn?*

4. *What are the developmental domains in a child?*

5. *What is Brain Based Learning?*

6. *Is knowledge of how the brain functions of any advantage in early childhood learning?*

7. *What are the differences between left and right brain dominant persons?*

The New Orientation in Childhood Learning

The new orientation in childhood learning is to help your child to be as efficient as possible in acquiring new information regardless of the contents of the domain. Emphasis is placed on making a child develop good thinking skills because it has been found that smart children are smart, "not by knowing all the answers but by being better thinkers" who are able to eliminate the wrong answer choices in a test. It was previously thought that all there was to learning was gathering information and storing them in our brains; now learning is considered to be "a dynamic process that helps you understand the universe". Children are born with an intense craving to understand their world. Another trend in learning is called Brain-Based Learning. This type of learning blends with the structure and functions of the brain. It is based on the concept that the left and right brains have different ways of processing thoughts and information during learning. The traditional way of learning has been found to use only half of the natural learning ability in a child since it utilizes the left brain mostly.

When Does Learning Start in a Child?

Real learning does not wait till a child enters school; discoveries from the science of early learning have found that children are born learning and this learning begins even before birth. Dr Charles Nelson, a neuroscientist at Harvard Medical School found that a child's brain patterns on scanning are different when hearing a "known" voice such as the voice of the mother which he or she has heard while in the womb. According to Jack P. Shokoff, MD- Samuel F and Rose B Gingold Professor of Human Development and Social policy, Brandeis University, "Young children from the beginning cannot help but learn. They don't have to be taught to learn; they are naturally wired up to learn. Right from birth, children are learning about the world. They are also learning about what learning is all about. So everything that is going on is a learning experience".

"There are only two things we should give our children. One is roots; the other, wings."

Hodding Carter

How Do Children Learn?

Children are active learners and the more involved they are in their own learning, the better they learn. The urge to learn in children derives from a desire to understand the world and their own experiences. Children learn the same way that scientists learn. They tinker with a lot of things just like scientists do with experiments and derive lots of fun from these after which they try to make sense out of their findings. This is the view of Alison Gopnik, D Phil. Professor of Psychology, Institute of Cognitive Sciences, University of California, Berkeley. **Social, emotional and intellectual learning all go together in children.** Social learning is what children learn from their important relationships such as parents, care givers and siblings. Emotional learning is what they learn when they are happy and feeling good and are engaged and motivated by what they are doing. Intellectual learning is what they gather from their attempts at making a sense of the world around them. According to Patricia K Kuhl, PhD, Professor of Speech and Hearing sciences, Co-Director, Institute for learning and Brain Science, University of Washington, "The brain is an interdisciplinary device. You can think of language, cognition and

social/emotional development as being totally separate, but that is not what the body provides evidence of. The baby is trying to map how people work, how the world works and does it as a composite. It's a multi-media event-that's what the world is and the brain maps it as a multi-media event, not separately". **What is an adult's role in a child's learning?** The role should be to encourage and increase a child's engagement in learning. An adult should resist the temptation of bombarding the child with factual information at every moment so that the child would not get over stimulated and develop phobia for learning. Children definitely need to learn some factual information such as colours, numbers and alphabets, however it should be done in an engaging manner, in a way that builds on the child's interests and extends the child's learning. According to Alicia F. Lieberman, PhD, the Johns Hopkins University Professor of Medical Psychology, "The motivation to learn comes from pleasure in learning, the joy in learning. When learning becomes a duty, the child rebels against it or gets bored with it".

Some Strategies for Promoting Early Learning in Children

Establish a loving relationship with your child. Good relationship is the engine of learning because it gives a child the confidence to go and explore the world; without it, very little development occurs in the child.

Observe your child at play while trying to understand and figure out what your child is working on. See the world through the eyes of your child and take notice of what he/she is curious about or trying to learn. Create room for learning through exploration, reflection, and imagination that occur during play and quiet times.

1. Make learning a joyful activity for your child and he/she will delight in learning. Encourage the natural drive in your child to overcome challenges.

2. Do not dampen your child's sense of curiosity, rather nurture it and keep it growing; it will make learning exciting for your child.

3. Make learning for your child focus on the here and now as a way of interacting with the world.

4. Go at the child's pace of learning and let the learning be about what interests the child. Do not compare your child with other children so that you would not put undue pressure on your child to learn.

5. Allow your child to learn in a hands-on way. Learning should help your child understand his or her experiences, not fill his/her head with facts in a "drill and kill" mode.

6. Give room for your child to create answers as he/she learns; resist telling the child the answer to his/her challenge.

7. Furthering your child's inquiries and building on his/her interests are the keys to maintaining interests in learning.

8. Aim at creating a balance between direct teaching and following the child's lead in learning if you are to sustain his/her interest in learning.

DEVELOPMENTAL DOMAINS OF A CHILD

The following are the developmental domains in a child:

Social Domain This is the ability to form attachments and play with other children. It also involves cooperation with other children, sharing and being able to create lasting relationships with others. According to Kathryn A. Hirsh-Pasek PhD, Professor of Psychology, Director, Infant Language Laboratory, Temple University "Research has found that children who make friends easily in kindergarten and are accepted by their classmates are also the ones who work hard in a self-directed way that fosters their academic competence".

Physical Domain-Development of fine and motor skills occur as the child grows. The child needs good nutrition because this is when the brain is developing most rapidly. Good health and adequate play opportunities help the child develop physically. Children of the same age differ in terms of the range of skills they can demonstrate and room should be given for individual variation.

Intellectual Domain—The child tries to make sense of the world around as he or she explores the environment.

Creative Domain-Development of talents such as music, art, writing, and reading comes from giving the child the needed attention for his/her talents to blossom.

Emotional Domain-Development of self-awareness, self-confidence and handling feelings occur as the child explores his surroundings. How the child sees himself, how she thinks, how he expects others to relate to him/her.

Cognitive Domain-This has to do with how children think, react and learn. Young children are capable and competent in learning irrespective of their background when given the necessary attention. Most of early life learning is acquired during play. The determinants of learning are the parents, the quality of the learning environment, the teachers/caregivers, challenging expectations as well as consistent guidance and mentoring. Knowledge of how children grow and develop together with expectations at their stage of development help in shaping the educational experiences of children.

BRAIN-BASED LEARNING

This type of learning uses strategies that are based on principles derived from an understanding of how the brain works. The brain is involved in everything a child does at home and at school while the activities of a child influence how the brain functions. The following are some of the principles behind this mode of learning:

1. Learning involves the whole person and encompasses both focused attention and peripheral perception. The brain has been found to function in such a way that it can perform several activities at the same time.

2. The search for meaning is innate and children go about it in their own way; patterning is the means by which children attain this goal.

3. Emotions are critical to learning; children learn better when they are happy and not under threat.

Learning involves both conscious and unconscious mechanisms.

4. There are broadly two types of memory; spatial and rote. We understand best when learning is embedded in our natural spatial memory.

5. Learning is enhanced by challenges and inhibited by threat. Let the learning environment immerse the child in an educational experience so that the child will have much to learn. Humor enhances learning in a great way.

6. Each brain is unique and processes information in wholes and in parts simultaneously. Teach your child different ways of solving problems; it's been found that children learn best when they are solving realistic not abstract problems.

7. Give room for the child to consolidate and internalize information by actively processing it. In learning, the big picture cannot be separated from the details.

8. Educators must be mindful of the fact that every brain is different; learners should be given room to know how they learn and should be able to customize their environment for effective learning.

9. Getting feedback from learners enables the educator to tailor the learning process to the child's needs.

'Life affords no greater responsibility, no greater privilege, than the raising of the next generation. "

C Everett Koop

What You Need to Know about the Human Brain

The following facts about the human brain help to establish the connection between it and learning:The ability of the human brain to grow new brain cells [neurons] are highly correlated with memory, mood and learning. Whatever aids the brain to form new cells promote learning. Neuroscientists like Gerd Kempermann and Fred Gage discovered that exercise, good nutrition and lower levels of stress promote the formation of new brain cells.

A school with good social environment positively impact on how the brain functions. Schools with good skill-building programs, reading, writing, music and arts courses, career and technical education, thinking skills etc, produce significant and positive changes in the brain of children. Gene expression had been known to up regulated in children attending such good schools. Chronic stress such as you have in abusive situations affects the brain adversely.

Articles in the Journal of Neuroscience and European Journal of Clinical Nutrition revealed that good nutrition promotes cognition, memory, attention and intelligence.

Exercise according to the Journal of Exercise, Paediatric Exercise Science and Journal of Exercise Physiology Online increases brain mass, better cognition and formation of new brain cells. Research has found that academic achievement is higher in schools where children have physical exercise than in schools without physical activities. Neuroscience has found exercise to increase the production of brain-derived neurotrophic factor which increases learning and memory capacity while reducing the incidence of depression in school children. Running has anti-depressive effects on children; in the United States where 1 in 6 teens makes plan for suicide, with roughly 1 in 12 teens attempting suicide, exercise improves the mental state of school children.

Right and Left Brain Dominant Persons

Split brain research carried out by Nobel Prize winner Dr Roger W Sperry in patients with severe epilepsy who had the tissues joining the two halves of the brain cut as treatment for severe epilepsy led to the discovery that the two halves of the brain function differently. The left and right brain are responsible for different modes of thoughts and the way a person thinks is determined by which side of the brain is used more often.

Right brain persons are more imaginative and intuitive by nature; they see things as a whole and are more interested in patterns, shapes and sizes. They exhibit artistic ability such as singing, painting, writing and poetry. They are described as divergent thinkers because they are creative and do not follow rules in expressing themselves. They excel in essay type questions as against left brained persons who do well in multiple choice tests.

Left brain persons are more logical and analytical in thinking; they excel in mathematics and work skills. They are called convergent thinkers because they follow the rules and are systematic in problem solving. They analyze situations to arrive at conclusion.

Every person uses both sides of the brain to function as normal persons, however the right brain absorbs new information in chunks while the left brain sifts and sorts it out in an organized fashion. Each side of the brain can do the other side's work, though not effectively. Right brain dominant persons spell poorly because they rely on intuition rather than follow the order in which letters in a word occur.

IMPLICATIONS OF BRAIN DOMINANCE THEORY ON EDUCATION

The educational system that emphasizes rote learning and strict adherence to syllabus encourages left brain use at the expense of right brain activity. Most examinations are designed to test left brain activity and they encourage conformity in thought; therefore left brain persons perform well in examinations. Right brain children do less well academically; they prefer group study activities and cannot sit still for long. They are more responsive in informal settings.

Teachers in the light of the brain dominance theory should see their class as a heterogeneous group of pupils with dissimilar interests and aptitudes and so should try to meet the needs of the different students.

Students should choose courses that are suitable to their learning style while aiming to strengthen other areas of their learning experience.

The methods of instruction should be such that appeal to a wide range of senses with a mixture of big picture and detail. Some students may choose to start learning with the big picture and work out the details later while some may prefer to start with the details and work up to the big picture.

A good school should have activities that appeal to and strengthen different styles of learning. Students should be assessed based on their learning styles while at the same time stimulating the different modes of learning.

IN A NUTSHELL

Getting involved in your child's education very early in life enables you to assess his/her learning ability and also to monitor his/her environment to see that it promotes learning. A safe stimulating environment would enable your child explore and learn.

1. Good nutrition and exercise help the brain of children to develop properly.

2. Brain-based learning is the latest frontier in learning; keeping abreast with developments in this field would enable you assist your child in developing sound learning skills.

LIFE APPLICATION

1. What learning strategies can you adopt to enhance your child's learning ability in line with what has been discussed in this chapter?

2. It would be good for you to observe your child at play, to know how he/she plays, what interests him/her and what you need to provide to enrich his/her play experiences.

3. Would you want to put your child in a better school where he/she would have

a good educational experience that will give him/her a head start in life.

FURTHER READING

R.W.Sperry; Brain Bisection and Consciousness in How the Self Controls its Brain, ed C. Eccles. Springer-Verlag, New York, 1966 S. Rose, The Making of Memory, Bantam Books, London, 1992

Ned Herrmann, The Creative Brain; Brain Books, Lake Lure, North Carolina 1990

B. Edwards, Drawing on the Right Side of the Brain, Fontana/Collins, 1982

Gerd Kempermann, Laurenz Wiskott and Fred Gage. "Functional Significance of Adult Neurogenesis". Current Opinion of Neurobiology, April 2004, pp186-91 Astrid Bjornbekk et al, "The Antidepressant Effect of Running is Associated with Increased Hippocampal Cell Proliferation". International Journal of Neuropsychopharmacology September 2005, pp 357-68

Mind in the Making: The Science of Early Learning

CHAPTER TEN
Improving Speaking and Listening Skills

FOCUSING QUESTIONS

1. *Why is it important for your child to improve on his/her speaking and listening skills?*

2. *What strategies can you use to help your child with these skills?*

3. *How would you develop public speaking skills in your child?*

4. *What are communication disorders?*

MILESTONES IN THE DEVELOPMENT OF SPEAKING SKILLS

Every normal child is born "hard wired" to communicate; the right stimulus which comes from nurturing and the environment would make the child talk as he grows. Babies resort to crying because they cannot speak when their diapers are wet or when they are hungry. Spoken words are the means through which growing children express themselves. From about nine months, a child can imitate sounds and respond to voices by cooing, gurgling and laughing. Toddlers [18 months to 36 months] can use one or two words to communicate their needs. As their vocabulary increases from interaction with their parents, other siblings and care-givers, they progress to using longer sentences like "Give me water' and other more descriptive languages. Pre-schoolers [3-5years] are able to express themselves and as they interact with their peers at kindergarten, their proficiency will increase.

"We make a living by what we get; we make a life by what we give."
Sir Winston Churchill

STRATEGIES FOR IMPROVING YOUR CHILD'S SPEAKING SKILLS

Children improve on their speaking skills depending on their mode of learning. The three types of learners are auditory learners, visual learners and physical learners.

Auditory learners learn more through what they hear and for such children you can improve their speaking skills by:

Be an active listener to your child. When he is speaking ask questions, ask him to make clarifications and pass comments that will encourage him to keep talking.

1. Converse with your child regularly. Talk on topics of diverse interests to you and your child. Such conversations will make your child ask questions or pass comments.

2. Always ask open-ended questions such as "What happened at school today" rather than "How was school today?" to which he/she may answer "Fine."

3. Do a recording of your child's voice while he is singing or telling a story. Play it back to him hearing and pay compliments. This will motivate your child to sing more often or talk better

while the recording serves as an oral portrait of your child at that age for keeps.

4. Read a story that is well known to him and deliberately introduce errors into the reading and ask your child to spot the errors and make the corrections. This will make him render the correct version of the story.

5. Ask your child to read at family devotions. Ask her to share what she has gained from the passage.

For a child who learns with his eyes i.e. visual learners, you can improve his speaking skills by:

1.Videotaping her while reading or telling a story. Play back the recording and she will be excited and would want to tell more stories. 2.Ask your child to describe an interesting movie he/she watched recently. This will encourage your child to speak.

Physical learners learn through action; they can improve their speaking skills by

1. Taking part in a family play or drama. This will make them talk.

2. Asking him to describe a city you visited during the last holidays.

3. Asking him to tell you a story which you will write down in a book for keeps. Periodically ask him to tell you stories you will document. This will act as stimulus for him to speak.

"If your children look up to you, you've made a success of life's biggest job."

Unknown

Developing Public Speaking Skills in Your Teenage Child

This skill is very important as recent polls in Europe and North America found that teenagers are more scared of public speaking than they are scared of death. This need not be so if they are equipped from home because skills learned at an early age easily assumes a second nature.

Benefits of public speaking skills.

1. It boosts self-confidence in a child when she can do whatever her peers are scared of doing. Because children are oblivious of how adults fear this exercise, they may see it as one of the rights of passage of growing up and easily acquire the skill.

2. Learning this skill early means having opportunities to practice extensively as the child grows up.

3. It makes the child comfortable at giving class presentation or demonstration when called upon to do so.

4. It makes the child a highly sought-after person to take part in plays and drama.

5. A child with a talent in oratory can begin to nurture this talent which is always in demand.

6. The child's mates would easily accept him as their leader because of this skill. He can easily become a first among his mates *[primus interperes]*

7. Children with such skills are not afraid of challenges.

8. Children with this skill are at an advantage when the time for employment comes. It enables you to give product

presentation for your company and also to deliver briefings in a professional manner. During training sessions at the workplace, the child stands out as a more articulate person.

STRATEGIES FOR HELPING YOUR CHILD DEVELOP PUBLIC SPEAKING SKILLS

A. Public Speaking Training at Home. Get your child to speak on an issue such as "How to care for a dog". Let him/her read up the subject and practice speaking before a dressing mirror.

Let the entire family be seated in the living room or at the dining table and listen to him/her with rapt attention. This simulates a formal setting. Let the session end with the audience [family members] asking questions and getting him/her to answer them.

B. Speaking opportunities at school. This may arise from contributions during class or if your child is a member of Literary and Debating club.

C. At Sunday school or bible study classes, he/she should be encouraged to speak or make contributions.

D. At birthday parties or social events. When there are opportunities for speeches, recitals or drama, encourage your child to make contributions.

LISTENING SKILLS

Before developing the ability to speak, babies build their knowledge of their environment through listening and observing. Through listening, they come to know the voice of their mother and her facial expression. Later on, a child is able to differentiate between voices, sounds and faces.

STRATEGIES FOR IMPROVING YOUR CHILD'S LISTENING SKILLS

The following strategies can be used:

Model listening to your preschool child by being a great listener yourself.

1. Ask him how his day went.

2. Maintain eye contact with your child while you are talking.

3. Give feedback to your child by repeating some aspects of his/her report.

4. Nod or use expressions like "aha" to show that you are listening.

5. Next tell him something interesting about your day and take him through the steps you used in listening to him.

For children in the elementary school or older children use these strategies:

1. Relate an incident to your child and deliberately pause to see if he would ask "What happened next?"

2. Teach how to take turns in listening and talking during a conversation. It prevents intrusion when another person is talking. You wait till the person speaking pauses before it is your turn to speak.

3. Be a great listener to your children. Don't have one ear glued to the TV while telling your child to "Speak on, I am listening".

CAUSES OF POOR LISTENING SKILLS

The following are some of the causes of poor listening skills:

1. Lack of training and instruction on how to listen. Children need to be taught this.

2. Distraction from Television while someone is talking.

3. Ear disorders that impair hearing.

4. External noise can serve as distraction.

5. Poor listening habits.

6. Attention deficit hyperactive disorder.

WHAT ARE COMMUNICATION DISORDERS?

These are disorders that impair a child's ability to speak. They are classified as:

Expressive Language Disorder when a child has developmental delay or difficulties in producing speech or

Mixed Receptive-Expressive Language disorder when a child has developmental delays and difficulties in the ability to understand spoken language and produce speech.

Such problems may be due to abnormalities of brain development, exposure to toxic substances such as lead while baby was in the womb or it could be genetic in origin.

A child with communication disorder may be unable to speak or have limited vocabulary for his age or have difficulties understanding simple instructions or is unable to name objects. Most children with delayed speech are able to speak at the time of starting school.

You may need to see a paediatrician or special education teacher or a speech/ language and mental health professional to know the exact nature of the problem.

There are two approaches to treating the condition. The remedial techniques employ increasing the child's communication skills in the area of deficit. The second approach helps the child build on his/her strengths to circumvent the communication deficit.

IN A NUTSHELL

1. Growing children express themselves through spoken words. Babies develop speech from crying, cooing, gurgling, to the use of one or two words in communicating at toddler stage to full blown speech in the preschool age.

2. Children are classified vide their mode of learning; they could be visual, auditory or physical learners. The child's mode of learning determines the strategy that will be useful in helping him develop speaking skills.

3. Public speaking skills can be developed as part of the rite of passage of a growing child.

4. Listening skills are needed by children to build their knowledge of the environment; you can model listening to your child by listening to him.

LIFE APPLICATION

Do you interact with your child in such a way as to promote his development of communication skills?

1. What class of learner does your child fit into?

2. What strategy would you employ to make your child develop public speaking skills?

FURTHER READING

WEB RESOURCES

American Speech-Language-Hearing Association www.asha.org

They provide information on early identification of speech and language delays and disorders, including signs that a child should be evaluated by a speech and language therapist.

Association for Childhood Education International [ACEI] www.udel.edu/bateman/acei

They provide information on Infant and Toddler Development and Education

CHAPTER ELEVEN
Developing Early Reading and Writing Skills

FOCUSING QUESTIONS

1. *Why are reading and writing skills important?*
2. *What strategies can you use to develop these skills in your child?*

THE IMPORTANCE OF EARLY READING SKILLS

Reading is an important milestone in the development of literacy in children. The earlier a child is able to read, the greater his interest in learning will be. Reading boosts a child's self-confidence while making him more inquisitive about the meaning of what he is reading. Early reading expands a child's vocabulary and makes the child develop interest in writing. Early reading promotes healthy social and emotional development in a child. It enhances imaginative and critical thinking skills which makes a child more aware of his environment. Early reading especially when brought about through the efforts of parents is associated with a sense of closeness and intimacy with the parent.

When a child reads early in life, she develops a long attention span that promotes better retention of information later in school. The enhanced memory and higher levels of concentration associated with early reading translates to better academic performance in life.

"One Father is worth more than a hundred schoolmasters."

George Herbert

INTRODUCING YOUR CHILD TO READING

Begin reading to your child in the early months of his/her life. The child would later come to associate books with the warmth of being held by you and the soothing sound of your voice. When your child sees reading time as fun time, you have succeeded in initiating him/her into a life time of reading and learning. Reading starts with letter knowledge; this is learning that letters are different from each other and that each has a specific name and a specific sound that goes with it. Get preschool books that deal with this and make your child know the alphabets.

Tools like plastic alphabets and Quercettic Magnetic letters greatly accelerate the acquisition of this skill. Allow your child play with these alphabets all over the house while teaching him at the same time.

1. Get your child to learn alphabet songs and nursery rhymes that teach knowledge of alphabets.

2. Help your child develop phonological awareness by making him play with the smaller sounds in words. The child gets to know that many words are made up of smaller sounds. Note that vowels are the hardest letter sounds for children to

learn because the sound varies with the usage of each vowel.

3. Build your child's vocabulary. Give him "words and their meanings" drill. The more words your child learns, the more connections he can make while reading and listening to stories. Deliberately choose books with new words to read to your child to arouse his curiosity.

4. Tell your child stories in a bid to teaching him how to tell stories. Get him to learn to describe things. Ask your child to retell jokes, stories and riddles.

5. Purchase a lot of story books for him and let him choose what to read at any particular time and for any length of time. A child may read a particular book over and over again without being bored.

6. Leave children's books lying all over the house so your child can pick and read as often as he likes.

7. Take your child on a visit to a library. This will create a strong positive impression about books and reading in him.

8. As he grows up and becomes more confident in reading, let him take turns in reading during family devotional reading from the Bible or any devotional

WRITING SKILLS

Writing is an important component of literacy. Children love to do what they see those around them do. They naturally take to scribbling on any paper or surface once they can handle any writing material such as pen, pencil or crayon. Writing and reading skills go together and compliment each other.

One known advantage of early writing skills is that it helps children develop small motor skills as they learn to manipulate writing materials and make controlled scribbling. Development of fine or small motor skills makes the child attempt things like using spoon to feed or putting on shoes by himself; activities that lead to self-sufficiency early in life.

STAGES OF WRITING DEVELOPMENT

Stage 1: Random Scribbling- for 2 and 3 year olds

Stage 2: Controlled scribbling-for 3 year olds

Stage 3: Letter like forms-3 and 4 year olds

Stage 4: Letter and symbol relationship-4 year olds

Stage 5: Invented spelling- 4 and 5 year olds

Stage 6: Standard spelling- 5 to 7 year olds

[Source: Macdonald S. (1997) The Portfolio and its use: A Road Map for Assessment. Southern Early Childhood Association

"Our greatest natural resource is the minds of our children."
Walt Disney

STRATEGIES FOR DEVELOPING WRITING SKILLS

1. Make available old newspapers, waste papers, jotters for scribbling and

drawing lines, shapes as first steps toward learning to write

2   Provide writing work books for guided practice as the child improves

IN A NUTSHELL

Early reading boosts a child's self-confidence, makes him more inquisitive, expands his vocabulary, and promotes healthy social and emotional development in the child.

1.   There are many activities that can help a child develop early reading skills.

2.   Early writing skills help your child develop small motor abilities which lead to self-sufficiency activities like self-feeding early in life.

LIFE APPLICATION

Develop the habit of reading to your child very early in life.

Invest in children's books for your child.

1.   Make efforts to see that your child develops writing skills early in life.

FURTHER READING

WEB RESOURCES

High/Scope Educational Research Foundation www.highscope.org

They are devoted to improving child development from infancy through adolescence.

Chapter Twelve
Learning Mathematics Early in Life

Focusing Questions

1. *Why is it important for your child to learn Math?*

2. *Why should parents be involved in teaching their child math?*

3. *What strategies can you use to help your child develop this skill?*

4. *What math activities can you do with your child?*

5. *Where can you get help when the need arises?*

The Importance of Mathematics

Mathematics is a subject that is put to use in everyday life; it is essentially the ability to reason and translate ideas into figures. There are abundant opportunities to hone this skill at home and make it fun before the child grows up to discover that children regard the subject as difficult.

Mathematics enables us handle everyday situations that involve numbers such as time to get to the birthday party, amount of money required for examination fees, distance to the grocery shop, etc.

Mathematics enables us to understand patterns which we see all around us. For example, office working hours is 7.30am to 3.30pm Mondays to Fridays. Mathematics improves your problem-solving skills and also helps you in making good decisions.

With mathematics, you are empowered to use modern technology such as computers and calculators to do computations.

It improves your budgetary ability which enables you to live within your means.

> **'By the time a man realizes that maybe his father was right, he usually has a son who thinks he's wrong.'**
>
> Charles Wadsworth

Why Parents Should Be Involved in Teaching Their Child Math?

The following are some of the advantages of parents getting involved in teaching their child math:

1. "Learning mathematics is a natural and developmentally appropriate activity for young children. From birth to age 5, young children develop an everyday mathematics including informal ideas of more and less, taking away, shape, size, location, pattern and position-that is surprisingly broad, complex and sometimes sophisticated"[H.P Ginsburg et al Social Policy Report: Giving child and Youth Development Knowledge Away Vol XX11, Number I 2008]

2. Teachers in most societies are poorly trained to teach this subject to very young children.

3. Many teachers lack knowledge of the subject and so cannot impart what they do not have.

4. Some teachers are afraid of the subject and so transmit this fear to their pupils.

5. Some teachers who do not know how important math subject is; and so teach it badly.

6. Low quality schools worsen the lot of children in mathematics because they have fewer lessons and poor supervision of the pupils; your child might have to fall back on what you taught him/her on the subject.

7. When parents are involved in teaching any subject, they tend to create moments to instruct their child often.

8. Mathematics ability upon entry to kindergarten is a strong predictor of later academic success and in fact is even a better predictor of early reading ability. [Duncan et al., 2007].

DIFFERENT METHODS OF TEACHING MATHEMATICS TO CHILDREN

This can be done in the following ways:

Allow your child to explore the environment Children learn through exploration. As your child plays with toys, you can begin to introduce mathematical concepts to his/her play.

Intentional Teaching for children of ages 3 to 6 This is a deliberate and planned instruction through which you introduce mathematical concepts, methods and language such as addition, subtraction, shapes etc, through a range of appropriate exercises. Such teaching sessions may last for 15 minutes.

Exploiting Teachable Moments in Everyday Activities. This is premised on cashing in on play activities of the child that are of teaching significance. You may ask your child to put biscuits or cookies one after another into a plate and count along. During play with Lego [plastic shapes], ask your child "what shape are you playing with"? "Is this shape bigger than that?" In this way you are introducing math into the child's play.

Geometry Exercises You may put different plastic shapes [circles, squares, rectangles and triangles] in a bag. Ask your child to close his/her eyes and take a dip and pick out a triangle. Make the child say why it is a triangle. This compels the child to think and analyze what a triangle is.

Interview Method. Stop your child in the midst of an activity of learning significance and ask the child the following questions:

"How did you do that?"

"Why are you doing that?"

"What's going on there?"

"Tell me what you are thinking about?"

The goal of questioning the child is to find out the thinking behind his present actions. As the child explains, math becomes a literacy activity because he is compelled to express himself. The child is hereby being exposed to the language function of math learning.

Means-End thinking Method This method assumes you can use what you have to get what you do not have. A child between 6 and 9 months uses this technique when he learns to pull the blanket closer to him in order to bring a toy within his reach. If you ask your child to bring 5 spoons and he gets 3 instead, ask him to go back and bring two more, in this way the child would be learning to count correctly.

Modeling Method A child playing with 3 blocks can be asked "If I give you two additional blocks, how many blocks will you have on the whole?" Again this is addition. Alternatively, a child playing with 5 blocks can be asked to remove 3 and now asked the number of blocks left.

Solving Problems Children above six years can improve on their math skills by solving a variety of math problems on a regular basis.

Trial and Error Older children also learn math by trial and error. It expands their reasoning horizon as they go about finding solutions to math problems. Through this, children learn that there may be more than one way of solving a problem.

Strategies for Helping Your Child Develop Mathematical Skills

1 Introduce your child to numbers

Children from ages 3 to 5 can be introduced to counting.

1. Make your child memorize numbers from 1 to 12 in words.

2. Next level for the child is to memorize numbers 13 to 19. Let your child know that these numbers are a bit unusual or irregular

3. Next level is to memorize 20 to 30 and this now follows a regular pattern.

Counting exercises may include asking your child to count the number of steps going up and down the stair; count the number of louver panes in your window, the number of doors in the house.

Use of counting songs such as "1, 2 buckle my shoes".

FOUR YEAR OLDS CAN LEARN TO COUNT 1 TO 100 BECAUSE IT HELPS THEM GET INTO PATTERNS IN A DEEP WAY.

2 Introduce your child to geometry

You can introduce children to geometry through use of plastic shapes [also known as Lego]. Show your child shapes of circle, square, triangle, etc. Even three year olds can be taught to name and recognize the differences. Let your child see the shape, name it and learn for instance that a triangle has three sides. Use geometrical expressions such as "pass me a cube of sugar". As part of play, make your child build structures with plastic blocks.

3 Introduce your child to Measurements

A child can be taught to measure the length of a stick with a tape rule. You can collect empty containers of various sizes and shapes. Let him compare their volumes by measuring the amount of water each jar can contain. Include children in

activities that involve measurement, for instance let your child note the amount of liters of fuel you bought into the car on your way home. Talk about time for school, time for favourite TV programmes.

4 Introduce your child to patterns

Your child is exposed to the first regular pattern that is seen in mathematics through counting. In this pattern, the child moves from 20 which is 2 tens to 30 [3 tens], 40

[4 tens] and so on and so forth. The tens have a pattern and after each ten you add 1, 2, and 3,4,5,6,7,8,9. The three levels of counting are: first simple memorization which takes the child from number 1 to 12; then memorizing in which the rules change and the child learns to count from 13 to 19 and the third is when the real mathematical pattern of base 10 is encountered.

Ability to recognize patterns helps us to make predictions based on our observation; understanding pattern helps a child get a good grasp of algebra in higher math class.

Look for patterns in story books, songs and poems where lines and sentences are repeated in predictable ways.

Explore patterns created by numbers.

Write the numbers 1 to 100 in rows of 10

1 to 10 in the first row

11 to 20 in the second row and so on and so forth.

Let the child observe how the numbers fall in the rows.

5 Introduce your child to data management

If you teach your child how to collect, organize and interpret data at an early age; he will develop the ability to manage information and make sound decisions in future.

Make a food chart in which the number of apples, oranges and tomatoes are recorded. Let him chart the number that is being consumed everyday.

6 Make math part of your child's day

You can do this as you show your child the many ways in which math is applied in everyday activities such making purchases from the grocery shop. You can also ask your child to name activities of the day where he employed math. Involve your child in domestic activities that involve math; for instance, "how many measures of rice would the house consume for lunch?"

Also do math problem with your child for the fun of it. Use calculator and rulers frequently in the home. Encourage your child to explain some of his action in math sense. Teach him to see incorrect answers to math problems as opportunities to learn something new.

"Every father is a hero in the eyes of his children"

Conover Swofford

HOW YOU CAN HELP YOUR CHILD IN ELEMENTARY SCHOOL OVERCOME CHALLENGES IN MATH

You may go about it this way:

1. Let your child know that every one can learn math, it depends on how determined and motivated you are to acquire the skill.

2. Let your child know that math is important even if his desire is a career in the humanities. Math can be fun if you choose to make it fun. Point out ways in which different family members use math in course of their jobs.

3. Be positive about your own math abilities. Avoid saying "I was never good in math" or "I never liked math". It might make your child feel his math

challenges were inherited and little can be done to improve his skills.

4. Encourage your child to be persistent when it comes to solving tough mathematical problems. He/she may take a challenging math problem to a peer or the math teacher for assistance. Tell your child that the more math problems he/she solves the greater his/her skills and confidence will be.

5. Praise him when he makes an effort and share in the excitement when he gets the solution to a problem.

6. You may get a math lesson teacher for your child if he needs helps on a regular basis till his skills improve.

IN A NUTSHELL

1. Mathematics is very important for everyday living. Early exposure of a child to mathematics dispels the fear usually associated with the subject because the child sees it as fun when the strategies listed in this chapter are used in teaching the subject.

2. Developing good mathematical skills early in life has been found to be a strong predictor of later academic success.

3. There are different methods by which mathematics can be taught to children in the home.

LIFE APPLICATION

1. In what practical ways have you tried to develop your child's interest in mathematics?

2 From what you have read in this chapter, what strategies are you going to employ to see that you child develops strong mathematical skills?

3 Do you have good books to assist you in teaching your child mathematics?

FURTHER READING

Social Policy Report: Giving Child and Youth Development Knowledge Away. Volume XXII, Number 1

Helping Your Child Learn Math. A Parent's Guide. Ontario Ministry of Education www.eqao.com

Early childhood Today Interview with Dr Herb Ginsburg on Math Education for Young Children- March 2009

CHAPTER THIRTEEN

Enhancing the Quality of Your Child's Education

FOCUSING QUESTIONS

1. *What is quality education?*

2. *Why does your child need quality education?*

3. *Are there research evidences of the benefits of Father Involvement in his child's education?*

4. *How can a father enhance the quality of education his child is getting?*

QUALITY EDUCATION

Quality education is not just the mere acquisition of knowledge but the training of the whole person-spirit, soul and body such that the person is able to locate his place in society. It is a system of learning that broadens the mind through mastery of what is being taught, acquisition of skills and change in behaviour. Education was cynically referred to as what is left after you have forgotten what you were taught at school; quality education aims to make what you have learned a part of you for life. Quality education creates in a person, a life long quest for knowledge. It has been said that over seventy five percent of university graduates never read a whole book for the rest of their lives after leaving school; quality education is the very antithesis of this mindset. It affects your behaviour positively and makes you an agent of change for the better in the society.

WHY DO CHILDREN NEED QUALITY EDUCATION?

Quality education enables children to think, interact, question and form concepts on their own in such way that they can live dignified and meaningful lives. It helps them seize the opportunities the information age offers in such a way that they enjoy the present while being equipped for the demands of tomorrow.

Children need quality education to be able to compete in the job market at this period of global economic gloom where unemployment rate is high. It guarantees a future of sustained economic and social capital in the workplace. It builds their self confidence and gives them an edge over their peers. It equips them with the necessary skills and capacities to succeed in life. The quality of life and aspirations of youth are compromised without quality education and training. Quality education makes learning interesting to the point of reducing drop-out rates and deviant behaviours among children.

> **"A man's children and his garden both reflect the amount of weeding done during the growing season."**
>
> Unknown

RESEARCH EVIDENCES OF BENEFITS OF FATHERS' INVOLVEMENT IN THEIR CHILDREN'S EDUCATION

The evidences include

1.The US Research Digest, Eric, found that even when fathers have limited schooling, their involvement in their children's schools and lives has a powerful impact on children's educational attainment. [Gasden, V and Ray, A (2003). Fathers' role in children's academic achievement and early literacy. Eric Digest, November]

A report that synthesizes data from two UK surveys on fathers' contribution to parenting and the effects of such contributions on their children's development found that there is a substantial increase in the amount of time parents devote to children in Britain, which has almost quadrupled since the 60's. Retrospectively, it was found that children who spent more than an average amount of time with their fathers in the 60's showed significant educational benefits, social and psychological adjustment later in life. [Fisher,K., McCulloch,A., & Gershuny, J. (1999). British Fathers and children: A report for channel 4 "Dispatches". University of Essex: Institute of social and Economic Research]

1. A survey of over 20,000 parents found that when fathers are involved in their children's education including attending school meetings and volunteering at school, children were more likely to get As, enjoy school, and participate in extracurricular activities and less likely to have repeated a grade.

Source: Fathers Involvement in their Children's Schools. National Center for Education Statistics. Washington DC: GPO, 1997.

25 PRACTICAL WAYS OF ENHANCING THE QUALITY OF YOUR CHILD'S EDUCATION

The following measures would yield good results:

A good father-child relationship is imperative. This would enable you create a partnership for learning with your child. He/she would readily divulge feelings or areas of frustration to you so that together you can work out solutions to the challenges.

Organize your home to support learning Talk positively about the value of education at home; celebrate learning and learned persons. This will create the right impression about learning in your child. Let a dictionary be always handy for your child to check out the meaning of new words. Always have newspapers around and discuss newsworthy events with everyone being encouraged to participate. **Expose your child to different study habits, methods and techniques.** Your child will be helped by knowing different ways of learning different subjects to gain mastery.

Teach him/her the basics of studying which are;

1. Employing all the senses: read it, say it, hear it, touch it and write it.

2 Read the subject regularly and frequently in other to move it from short to long term memory.

3. Organize the facts in such a way as to make it easy to recall

4. Create lists and use mnemonics to remember them.

5. Create flash cards for easy revision.

6. Write study notes to augment what your lecture notes contain.

7. Create charts to illustrate facts

8. Make jigsaws; pin on labels to study diagrams and maps.

9. Learn to link facts in a way that makes it easy for you to remember them.

The SQ4R method is another acclaimed method of studying. The acronym describes the various steps in this method of study.

1. S stands for survey of the subject- get an overview of what you want to study such as the contents, headings, and graphs etc,

2. Q stands for questions-change the chapter and subheadings to questions so you can attempt to conjecture what you are about to read

3. R stands for read-attempt to answer the questions as you read

4. R stands for recall- try to remember what you have just read

5 [R]W Write down the major points you wish to remember

6 R-review all you have read, make inputs from what you have read else where.

Kumon method of learning Mathematics. This is a Japanese system of learning mathematics that is based on repetition and practice with pupils spending a little time every day working on sums. It is built on the maxim that 'practice makes perfect'. It helps in boosting the potential of each child by building his/her self confidence.

The Abacus Method of learning mathematics. This method enables children at an early age to acquire the ability of calculating rapidly and accurately as well as being to calculate mentally. This proficiency in mental calculation comes from their use of the abacus image which allows quick calculation without actually using abacus.

Listen to your child talk about his learning process. Do not convey the impression of "Do as I tell you", "I am in charge here". Comment on his moods especially if he feels down cast. Look for shared interests in learning that you can dialogue on. **Encourage self-directed learning** This is learning that is self-initiated. It is a good way of overcoming learning challenges which could discourage him. A lot of learning in life after school comes from self-directed learning. Self directed learning has the following advantages:

1. It makes your child the owner and manager of his/her learning process because it combines self-management with self-control. In essence, it creates autonomy in learning.

2. It shifts the control of learning from teachers and parents to your child because he can exercise independence in what he wants to learn from beginning to the end. It makes your child willing and curious to learn new things on his own.

3. Your child comes to the self-awareness that it is his responsibility to make learning fun, meaningful and with the power to monitor himself.

4. Your child becomes more effective in learning and is able to identify and

befriend his/her peers that share similar interests.

5. Your child will be able to search for information on several topics from a wide variety of sources using different strategies and end up storing the information in a way he/she can easily retrieve.

6. You encourage your child to do self-learning by letting him know about his role in acquiring knowledge while giving him the free hand to pursue subjects of his own interest.

Judicious and Constructive Use of the Internet The internet is a huge library that brings information to a person's fingertips. Teach your child how to source for information on the net while resisting the time-wasting distraction it could constitute for a person without self-control.

Be involved in your child's learning at home Read to your child while he is young; help him through his homework in the preschool and elementary school level. Help him establish a culture of doing his home work before play or TV watching.

Monitor his progress at school Visit his school, get to know his school environment, talk to his teachers, and attend the parents-teachers association meetings. This will enable you relate to issues that concern your child's education properly.

Create family learning activities Games like scrabble, mathematic quiz, jigsaw puzzles, and other games of similar genre have a way of boosting learning. Use every avenue to make learning fun in the home.

Use curiosity and desire to motivate your child to learning You can introduce a topic that is unknown to him but which he would find interesting such as Robotic Surgery or Astronomy. Ask him to read it up and then share his findings with you. In this way, he will feel competent and in control of his life. **Give praise and support to your child when he excels in his studies.** This will motivate him to work harder. Speak positively of your expectations of him. Children have a way of working hard not to disappoint loving parents. **Be careful of what you use in rewarding academic success.** Researches had found that children who learn to get good grades or to be rewarded tend to stop learning once they have attained their goals. Let the goal of learning be to master a topic because one day, this knowledge will be useful to me or to society.

Make your child see learning as a life-long process. In this way, he will eagerly update himself on the recent development in his field of knowledge. Let him know that there is no retirement from learning; rather he should continue to improve on himself. **Use fiction, non-fiction, and recreational materials to share knowledge in the home.** Such informal settings can be put to learning advantage since so many of such opportunities abound in a regular home. **Use experiences to teach** When a child does very well in his examinations through dint of hard work, let him see the link between hard work and result. He will put in more efforts to get good grades. **Send your child to good schools** Such schools are expensive especially when they combine training in values with academics. Make the financial sacrifice; you will see that it was worth it later in life. **Encourage your child to fraternize with peers of similar**

interest in learning. A person who shares your interest will encourage you in your learning pursuit and will quite often support you with books and his experiences.

Buy or borrow books for your child Aside from recommended books which you should buy for your child, other books which his teacher feels would help him should be made available to him. You can also make available to your child books on general knowledge as well as fiction books to broaden his knowledge.

Restrict lessons to subjects which are challenging to your child. This leaves your child with enough time to study, do his homework and have time for recreation. In Nigeria of today, taking lessons whether necessary or unnecessary has become the greatest hindrance to self-directed learning because it wears the child out and gives a false impression of hard work.

Let your child watch educational TV programs. The saying of "Not throwing away the baby with the bathwater" can be extended to watching television by your children, Tele programs like those on Discovery channels greatly broaden the scope of knowledge of children by letting them know things that are beyond the scope of regular school syllabus. **Participation in co-curricular activities** Such as membership of press club, literary and debating society, dramatic society, scout movement, girls' guild, geographic society, etc. They not only broaden the knowledge of children but also equip them with vital skills that will make them stand out in life.

Good habits Such as listening to radio especially stations like Nigerian Broadcasting Corporation, British Broadcasting Corporation, Voice of America, etc, etc. Your child will learn new words and right pronunciations in addition to new knowledge. It will help his spoken English greatly. Let him have his own radio for this purpose. **Group learning with peers of shared interests.** This will bring cross-fertilization of ideas concerning different subjects. It will also provide mutual support for members of the learning group.

Visits to citadels of learning, libraries and notable places like Aso Rock, White House, State Governor's house etc, etc, This could have a salutary effect on your child that will make him aim very high in life if he has opportunities to visit such places. Since learning is the passport to great achievements in life, he will work to achieve his academic goals in life. **Encourage him to develop writing skills** Let him learn to write articles for his school magazine or press club. It helps him search for knowledge as well as help him in self-expression. So many people make a living out of writing. **Improve your child's thinking skills.** Teach him how to think constructively. Come up with ways of developing and strengthening his biological instruments of learning; the senses [entry point of information] and the brain which is the processing and storage centre of the body. This topic is well covered on the chapter on critical thinking.

"If you want children to put their feet on the ground, put some responsibility on their shoulders."
Abigail Van Buren

IN A NUTSHELL

Quality education empowers your child to seize the opportunities life will offer him to be successful.

1. A father's involvement in his child's learning brings about better learning outcomes, social and psychological adjustment in later life.

2. There are many strategies by which a child's learning can be enhanced.

LIFE APPLICATION

1. Evaluate the educational attainment of your child vis a vis his class or grade. How would you rate his performance using the following grades- Excellent, Good, Average, Poor?

2. Which of the strategies list in the chapter would you want to use to assist your child?

3. What are the learning challenges militating against your child attaining his educational goals?

FURTHER READING

ICTs for Education: A Reference Handbookhttp://www.ictinedtoolkit.org.

PART FOUR:
INSTILLING MORAL AND ETHICAL VALUES INTO YOUR CHILD

"Choose my instruction rather than silver, and knowledge rather than pure gold. For wisdom is far more valuable than rubies. Nothing you desire can compare with it."

Proverbs 8:10-11

"The only thing that walks back from the tomb with the mourners and refuses to be buried is the character of a man. This is true. What a man is survives him. It can never be buried.".

R. Miller

CHAPTER FOURTEEN

Developing a Personal Value System

FOCUSING QUESTIONS

1. *What is a Personal Value System?*

2. *Why does your child need a Personal Value System?*

3. *What are the values that should be part of your child's Personal Value System?*

4. *What are the determinants of the Personal Value System of a child?*

5. *What is the role of the Father in determining the Personal Value System of his child?*

WHAT IS A PERSONAL VALUE SYSTEM?

A personal value system is the set of values a person considers important and desirable enough to want to acquire and make the guiding principles of life. A child must have his/her independent convictions regarding moral, ethical, spiritual and social issues as she transits from childhood to adulthood; this is where the need for a personal value system becomes obvious.

WHY DOES A CHILD NEED A PERSONAL VALUE SYSTEM?

The following are the reasons why your child needs a personal value system:

It defines his/her person's character and what he/she stands for. If among his peers, your son is known for truthfulness, he would not agree to collaborate in an examination malpractice. His mates who planned to cheat would not bother to enlist him in their plans.

It provides a guide for living; it is a compass for locating one's self in society Developing autonomy in this area is crucial to his/her evolving into a responsible law abiding citizen. A child that has imbibed good moral values before leaving home for the University would most likely continue on this path if he has strong convictions about the values he holds dear in life.

A child becomes more self-aware pertaining to what he/she can and cannot do. If a girl with good moral values is asked to read a pornographic magazine, she will most naturally turn it down because it conflicts with her core values.

It imparts credibility to your child She will be respected among her peers as a trustworthy person who will not indulge in despicable acts. **It helps a child make ethical decisions fast.** Becoming a cult member will not hold attraction for a boy or a girl with good personal value system. Such an individual would turn down without equivocation any invitation to join a cult.

It determines the choice of friends The bible in Amos 3:3 says "two cannot walk together unless they agree". A child with good personal value system will always consider it an unholy alliance to be a close friend to a perpetual law-breaker. **You know**

people's expectations of you This makes a child careful in all his ways especially in making his actions congruent with his value system. **He/she will be considered a principled person** When your child acts consistently in line with values she holds dear, she will be considered a principled person who can be entrusted with great responsibilities. She will stand out among her peers.

It can determine a career choice Your child would likely not consider a career in which his/her personal value system would be compromised.

23 DESIRABLE VALUES FOR A PERSONAL VALUE SYSTEM

Godliness This is a lifestyle of walking according to the precepts of God as spelt out in the bible. It is a life patterned after Christ that celebrates everything that is good. **Respect** This value will make you give people the honour that is their due especially parents, teachers, employers and all those in position of authority. It is always a compliment to be described as a respectful person who respects both lowly and highly placed persons. **Selflessness** This value is the very antithesis of selfishness. A person with this virtue never considers personal gain when handling an issue. He never gets interested on any issue because of what he stands to gain.

Love This value makes you wish others what you want done to you. He always wishes his neighbour well. A loving person does kind acts without thinking of getting anything back. **Integrity-**this is wholeness in every aspect of your life. Your word is your bond while your actions always conform to the perception people have of you and the values you are known for. A person of integrity will always say the truth even if the heavens will fall. **Truthfulness** The act of always saying the truth and abiding by it. Growing up we had this common expression; "Say the truth and let the devil be ashamed".

Honesty This is always considered the best policy. It is the act of presenting issues the way they are without any intent on deceiving the hearers. An honest person will rather fail than cheat in an examination; over invoicing or falsifying account data is anathema to an honest person.

Contentment This is a condition of being satisfied with your lot in life. It does not preclude a person from aspiring for higher office in life; rather the person goes about it in a legitimate way. There is no desperation in trying to get the good things of life. The apostle Paul told Timothy in **1Tim 6:6 "But godliness with contentment is great gain"**. **Sincerity** This has to do with presenting yourself the way you are without intending to give a different impression of your person. A sincere person says what he means and means what he says. **Courage** This is boldness to do what needs to be done at any particular time. It might demand saying things that everybody knows but nobody is bold enough to address the matter. You need courage to be your own person in this decadent society.

Persistence or Tenacity of Purpose This value is common among all those who at one time impacted their generation. The life of Abraham Lincoln epitomized this virtue:

At the age of seven, a young boy and his family were forced out of their home. The boy had to work to support his family. At the age of nine his mother passed away. When he grew up, the young man was keen to go to law school, but had no education.

At 22, he lost his job as a store clerk. At 23, he ran for state legislature. He lost. At 31, he was defeated in his attempt to become an elector. By 35, he had been defeated twice while running for congress, but at 39 he lost his re-election bid.

At 41, his four-year old son died. At 42, he was rejected as a prospective land officer. At 45, he ran for the senate and lost. Two years later, he lost the vice presidential nomination. At 49, he ran for the Senate and lost again.

At 51, he was elected the President of the United States of America. he man in question was Abraham Lincoln.

Unknown Author

Patience This is the ability to wait till what you desire or wish gets to you. Get rich quick syndrome has wrecked the testimony of many otherwise decent persons. **Kindness** This is the ability of meeting another person's needs at your own expense. It usually flows from a tender hearted person. **Accountability** This is the ability to account for what has been committed into your care. It is also the ability to hold yourself responsible for your actions instead of saying "The devil made me do it". An accountable person is a disciplined person who will not misuse whatever is committed into his/her care. Such persons are highly sought after for leadership positions. **Dependability** You can be counted upon; you are not a traitor. **Loyalty** You are a faithful person who will not betray any trust confided in you. You will not stab an unsuspecting friend at the back. **Humility-** This is one virtue that accentuates greatness. You do not sing your own praises or talk about your achievements. You consider others to be better than yourself and you show it in your dealings with people. You accord persons the respect that is their due.

Modesty This is a mindset of not disclosing your achievement in life; "you do not blow your own trumpet"

A Forgiving Heart The aphorism, "to err is human but to forgive is divine" describes the nobility of this virtue. Such a person always makes allowances for the shortcoming of others and is ever willing to extend forgiveness to those who are unrepentant of their evil actions. **Justice, Equity and Fairness** This has to do with giving people their due or what they deserve. This virtue makes a society live able for every class of persons.

"**The simple exercise of praying together regularly as a family will do more to strengthen your family than anything else you could do together.**"
Bruce Bickel and Stan Jantz

WHAT DETERMINES THE PERSONAL VALUE SYSTEM OF YOUR CHILD?

The personal value system of your child is determined by: **Your lifestyle** The way you live your life communicates very loudly to your child and he would likely follow in your footsteps unless there is some intervention. Speak to your son about good values early in life and try to live out these values in his presence. When you ask your child to tell a lie to a visitor you do not wish to see, that you are out of the home while you are actually at home, you are teaching your child to lie.

Your input into his life This is a deliberate effort on your part to nurture or put these values into your child. When your child comes home from school with a pen that belongs to his mate, tell him that it is a thief that takes what belongs to others. The following day, make him return the pen to the rightful owner and he will learn what honesty is all about. When you do not permit swear or curse words at home, your child will cultivate decent diction.

The home environment A home where dishonesty is freely practiced will support a child who wants to cheat at examination. **Experiences in life** A child who shoplifted and was made to return the stolen items to the shop owner will not forget easily the embarrassment of admitting that he/she stole. Such a child will avoid taking what belongs to others another time.

The school environment A child spends so much of his/her time at school while growing up. At school he comes under the influence of his peers for better or for worse. Put your child in a school that would build on the good values he is getting from home. Such schools are usually costlier than public schools; however the difference they make in the lives of your children cannot be quantified. A school that supports examination malpractices short changes your children for life becomes it sentences

them to mediocrity rather than training them to be true achievers.

The company he keeps Ensure your child keeps good company because bad company corrupts good morals. Ask your child to invite his friends home, interact with them and advise your children accordingly. Teach your child what to look for in his peers that will make good friends.

Reading good books Have a library of good books or story books that have strong moral lessons in them. Subscribe to magazines that will teach your children about the Bible, the ultimate book on godliness. Let them have their own devotionals. Have a time to discuss on a one-on-one basis what each child learned from his/her book.

Warn your child about the hazards of pornography. Pornography is a multibillion dollar industry that seeks to debase the morality of your child. It is not only addictive; it ultimately leads to premarital sex and teenage pregnancy that leaves lasting scar on your child. Don't wait for him to discover this by himself. It may be late before you get to know.

Let your child join groups, societies or clubs that would influence his morals for good. Christian groups have a lot to offer young persons regarding moral values; encourage your child to be involved in them. Movements such as Scout and Girls' Guild have for years been the bastion for forming the character of young persons; encourage your child to join one of them.

Limit time spent watching TV and surfing the Net So many of what is shown on the TV neutralizes the moral values you are trying to build into your child. Censor the programs they watch and help them to differentiate good from bad programs. Time wasted on TV cannot be regained while a life spent on watching make-belief stories is a time wasted. Programs with high moral contents can be helpful to children. Violent films teach children aggression and should be discouraged. Serial soap operas have longed been acknowledged as time wasters.

Censor the music he listens to Music has powerful influence over children and youths. Be sure the lyrics of his music builds on the moral values you are teaching your child. Explain to him what bad music can lead to.

"You've got to do your own growing, no matter how tall your grandfather was."

Irish Proverb

15 Practical Measures to Impart Good Personal Value System To Your Child.

1. Pray for him that he would choose the path of righteousness as against perversity.

2. Get a copy of the bible for him/her as well as a daily devotional to stimulate his faith. The bible says in **Ps 119: 9, 11**

   'How can a young man cleanse his way? By taking heed according to your word'.

   Your word have I hidden in my heart, that I might not sin against you'.

   3. Tim 3:15-16 'All scripture is given by inspiration of God, and is profitable for doctrine, for reproof, for correction, for instruction in righteousness, that the man of God may be complete, thoroughly equipped for every good work'.

   Make sure he attends church and is involved in the activities of the church.

4. Get to know his friends since bad company corrupts good morals.

5. Be a warm, open, loving and approachable father, be consistent and fair in your rules. Talk to your child always about good values in life and be an example to him in righteous living.

6. Give your child graded responsibilities that involve decision making in the home. Discuss the outcome with him.

7. Create opportunities for open discussion on moral issues, scriptural issues and politics. Guide him in forming his opinions.

8. Look for opportunities to talk about the consequences of good and bad behaviour.

9. Hold your child accountable when he makes a poor choice so that he can experience the connection between behaviour and consequences.

10. Enroll him in fellowships, clubs or societies that have a lot to offer on morals.

11. Buy good books for him.

12. Get good films as a substitute for bad films for him.

13. Censor the music he listens to because it has a powerful influence over him.

14 Get him involved in social service or volunteer work that will create a social conscience or awareness in him.

15 Plant the seed of generosity in him by making him give to the poor and needy; in this way when he becomes involved in social service in future, he would be accountable.

IN A NUTSHELL

1. Your child needs a good personal value system to enable him survive in this morally decrepit world.

   Through different practical ways, you can help him develop a good value system.

LIFE APPLICATION

Have a one-on-one discussion with your child on the topical issues of the day such as examination malpractice, cultism, drugs, internet fraud, premarital sex and teenage pregnancy. Find out his views and see ways in which you can help him strengthen his convictions if he is on the right.

FURTHER READING

Gibbs, J.C. (2003) Equipping Youth with mature Moral Judgment. *Reclaiming Children and Youth,* Vol. 12 no. 3 fall 2003. pp 148-153

Chapter Fifteen
Character Modeling

Focusing Questions

1. *What is Character?*

2. *Why is character important?*

3. *What is the role of the family in character development?*

4. *In what ways can a father help in the character formation of his child?*

5. *In what ways can the government promote good character development?*

What Is Character?

Character is who you are or the type of person you are. It is a pattern of positive and negative behaviour that describes a person. It is the inner workings of a person that govern his/her actions and make him/her a unique individual. Attributes such as integrity, fidelity, honesty, courage, justice, patience, industry and modesty describe a person's character. Success at self-regulation is the hallmark of a good character, and this is best learned in the early years of life especially from the hands of parents. Testifying before the US House Education and Workforce Committee at the Capitol on 28/6/06, Jack Nicklaus, the legendary golfer said, "Every child needs a grounding and positive reinforcement at home and at school so that they can learn respect, courtesy, responsibility and other core values".

Nature Versus Nurture in Character Development

Character is made not born; it is determined by both nature and nurture. Nature is what a child is born with and is inherited through genes from both parents. Nurture on the other hand is acquired behavioural traits that come from the environment such as the home, school, church, society and peer influence. A child may be very active and daring by nature; however through nurturing such a child can become calmer and graceful. Likewise naturally born introverts can under environmental influence become friendly, out going persons. Stephen Scott, a professor of child health and behaviour at King's College London, conducted a range of studies where he established a link between parental influence and genetic predisposition in shaping the character of a child. He says "There's an interaction between your genetic predisposition and the way you turn out according to the way you are raised. When it comes to being antisocial, aggressive, stealing and lying, the interaction is a big one. If you have poor self-control and a rather twitchy, irritable temperament and you're brought up in a bad way, its bad news. For that group, the rate of criminality for that age 17 is about 40 per cent. But if you have that twitchy character and you are brought up in a reasonably calm, soothing way----your parents don't overreact, they let you run around in the park after school---you will do well". In forming the character of your child, consider his strengths and weaknesses and raise him/her accordingly.

WHY CHARACTER IS IMPORTANT

Character is an old idea with a contemporary relevance; children who inherit great wealth from their parents but lack character will not make much of their advantage; they will gravitate towards poverty. A poor start in life in terms of character development impairs educational performance which in turn limits job opportunities.

The importance of character cannot be overemphasized since the defining qualities of a good character are of vital importance in the construction of a successful life. A famous Yale professor in a discussion with Theodore Roosevelt, a former US president about Yale and Harvard football teams made this remark about a certain player in the Yale team: "I told them not to take him, for he is slack in his studies, and my experience is that, as a rule, the man who is slack in his studies will be slack in his foot-ball work; it is character that counts in both". The character of a person more than anything else reveals the nature of the person and the principles by which such a person lives his/her life. Robert Baden-Powell, the founder of Scouts movement had in mind the formation of young men who will be distinguished by "the spirit of self-negation, self-discipline, sense of humour, responsibility, helpfulness to others, loyalty and patriotism, all of which go to make character".

Children who do not possess good characters are at a disadvantage when they go to the labour market; they simply do not get hired and life's chances tend to slip out of their hands. The net effect of this is social immobility and a sentence to a life of mediocrity.

There is a shift in today's economy towards service jobs where the character of the worker is paramount and the emphasis is on employing "nice persons". Persons who possess "soft skills: such as social skills, patience and courtesy will be preferred to those who lack such skills.

"Character is largely caught, and the father and the home should be the great sources of character infection".

Frank H Cheley

CONTENTS OF A GOOD CHARACTER

Persons of good character are always in high demand because society is ever often in short supply of them. Richard Reeves, Director of Demos, UK, described the three key ingredients of character as: a sense of self-direction, an acceptance of personal responsibility and effective regulation of one's emotions in particular the ability to resist temptation or delay gratification. A person of good character will display honesty, integrity, trust dependability, hard work, responsibility and moral strength in all his/her dealings.

THE ROLE OF THE FAMILY IN CHARACTER DEVELOPMENT

The family plays an important role in the development of a child's character. The two adult parents' families with older siblings who are well behaved provide the ideal environment for character development. Through routine family activities such as meal times, family vacations, devotion and recreation times, tit bits of what makes a solid family is both observed and transmitted to the children. Parental authority when exercised especially when the child is young goes a long way in forming the child.

Studies have shown that low income families measure poorly when it comes to raising children with good character. The root cause of this is not finance; rather it is poverty of the parent-child experience. Consistent parental love and discipline which drive the motor of the character production line is often lacking in these families. Well groomed children are always at an advantage when they get to the job market.

The social liberalism of this age characterized by endless hours spent watching TV, internet, ready availability of alcohol; drugs and pornography conspire to corrode the character of children. Parents who spend long time away from home on account of their jobs leave their children at the mercy of these negative influences.

Parents must exorcise the spirit of individualism that typifies this age because it crowds out the quest for virtue and morality in impressionable children.

Parents have a duty to mitigate the consequences of the loss of regulation of public behaviour that leaves the child without moral reference points. Parents must budget time, energy and commitment to their children for an average of twenty years per child if their children are to be endowed with good character.

Parents who did not have solid home experiences or who feel inadequate in parenting should attend parenting classes where ever these are held. Such classes have been found to fill in gaps in the act of parenting. Stephen Scott, a director of research and development at the National Academy of Parenting Practitioners attests to the efficacy of these classes from the result of a ten-year study which shows that between one third and one half of the improvements in parental performance after classes remain a decade after the intervention. Parents should send their children to schools which will add value to the lives of their children in this regard. Sunday school classes of different churches also provide valuable inputs in the development of character of children. Encouraging children to join clubs and societies that emphasize good character development adds to what children get from home. A movement such as Scout was able to impart so many youths because it provided regular time with same adult over a long time period so that a relationship that is founded on respect for the adult was formed and this aided mentoring.

HOW A FATHER CAN HELP HIS CHILD DEVELOP GOOD CHARACTER

Children need their parents' input to develop into responsible adults. Oscar Wilde, the Irish poet and dramatist has this to say of youth; ***"Youth! There is nothing like youth. The middle-aged are mortgaged to life. The old are life's lumber room. But youth is the Lord of life. Youth has a kingdom waiting for it.***

Everyone is born a king, and most people die in exile". Without character, a young person stands a narrow chance of being a success in the corporate world and may never be upwardly mobile.

HE MUST BE AN EXAMPLE OF ALL HE WANTS HIS CHILD TO BE IN LIFE

The bible says 'train up a child in the way he should go and when he is old, he will not depart from it' [Proverbs 22:6]. Abraham Lincoln said, 'the only way a Father can train a child in the way he should go is for him to walk the way'. Children learn more by observing what their parents do than from what they are taught. Make sure you are an example in truthfulness, honesty and fair play in all your dealing; then it becomes easy for your child to understand the importance of these values in real life.

CREATE A TIME FOR SPECIFIC INSTRUCTIONS ON CHARACTER BUILDING VALUES

Let a portion of your family devotion be dedicated to moral instruction. A chapter a day from the book of Proverbs in the Bible will give enough food for thought on values that build character. The whole book of proverbs will take the family 31 days if read a chapter a day after which another book of the bible that dwells on character building values can be taken. Books other than the bible that offer moral lessons can also be read from time to time. According to C.S. Lewis: "Human beings must be trained in obedience to moral intuitions almost before they are rational enough to discuss them, or they will be corrupted

before the time for discussion arrives". Teach your child and take time to explain to him the morality of certain actions.

"Character may be manifested in the great moments, but it is made in the small ones".

Phillips Brooks

USE OF WISE SAYINGS, PRUDENT MAXIMS AND MORAL SENTENCES

These power packed sayings have a way of leaving strong and lasting impressions on the memory of young persons.

USE ANECDOTES TO TEACH MORAL LESSONS

Society never lacks anecdotes that pack enough punches to educate young minds. The Enron scandal would provide valuable lessons in corporate fraud. Enron was a multinational corporation which grew from nowhere to be America's 7th largest company in 15 years. It had 21,000 staff in its payroll in more than 40 countries. However, investigations will later reveal that its success was an elaborate scam woven around lies about their profitability and concealed debts which were not reflected in the company's audited accounts. The company declared bankruptcy in 2002 while those found guilty were sent to jail. It teaches us that there is nothing hidden that will not be revealed; therefore honesty remains the best policy. There are always lessons in everyday life and in the dailies which a discerning father can use to build his child's character.

CREATE ETHICAL BOUNDARIES FOR YOUR CHILD

Let there be sanctions for telling lies to discourage children from this vice which is a gateway to other vices. Use your child's mistakes and wrong actions as opportunities to teach him what proper action is and use it to form his character.

BE PROACTIVE

Consider the uniqueness of your child and make an inventory of his/her character needs rather than his/her faults; you will be in a position to employ rational means in building a good character in him/her.

USE ORAL HISTORY

Extended family members suffering on account of their character flaws might be used as ready examples to discourage your child from walking in their footsteps. There may be some family members who because of laziness ended up being poor or doing low paying jobs. My father taught me early in life that laziness is one ailment that the physician has no cure for, because it is a mindset that paralyzes the rest of the body. Use stories of persons your children know or whom they can relate to in conveying moral lessons. With stories and anecdotes, you are creating a memory bank in your child that he will draw upon in building his character.

KNOW YOUR CHILDREN'S FRIENDS

The trite saying of "Show me your friends and I will tell you who you are" comes handy in describing a child's character and tendencies. Teach your child how to know good boys and how to be friendly with such persons. Teach him to shun the company of boys who always get into trouble at school. Ask him to invite his friends home so you can interact with them and know about their background. Because bad company corrupts good morals, it is never too early to alert your child about the dangers of peer influence.

BEHAVIOURAL CHANGES

Character training entails weaning your child off unwholesome habits. A child who steals can be told the consequences of stealing especially using everyday examples. Attitudinal changes will be demanded while counseling is sought if need be.

ALLOWING YOUR CHILD FACE THE CONSEQUENCES OF HIS/HER ACTIONS

If your child shoplifts and you discover it at home, explain to him/her while that act is reprehensible. Make him/her take the stolen item back to the shopkeeper as soon as is possible with apologies to the shopkeeper. The gut-wrenching fear, shame and guilt with the uncertainty of the outcome of returning a stolen item are a enough to serve as deterrent for such a child. Making a child apologize to those has wronged makes the child more careful in his utterances and actions. Long term consequences of certain actions may not be lost on children. A child caught cheating during an examination might be labeled a cheat. Much later in life, if he seeks a political or public office, his school mates who were aware of his misdemeanor can embarrass him with that record.

DISCIPLINARY MEASURES

The cane still has a place in shaping the character of some children, but must be used only when other measures had failed. The book of proverbs says; "Foolishness is bound up in the heart of a child, but the rod of correction will save thc child". There should be different disciplinary measures that match the offence; measures could range from denial of privileges to corporal punishment. Restitution by doing some odd jobs in the home for specific offenses also drives home the message that the consequences of wrong doing goes beyond the offender to affecting the larger community.

COMPASSION

Teach your child compassion and empathy by making him show compassion to less privileged persons. Encourage him to participate in volunteer services for the less privileged.

WHAT GOVERNMENT CAN DO TO PROMOTE GOOD CHARACTER DEVELOPMENT IN THE SOCIETY

A nation is as strong as the moral character of her citizens; because of this the issue of character development should occupy a front burner in the programme of government. Government can assist parents by doing the following:

1. Establishing a strong criminal justice system where persons who run fowl of the law are duly punished. This will serve as deterrent to those with criminal tendencies. Nobody should be above the law when it comes to dispensation of justice.

2. Persons who exhibit good character should be celebrated and held up as role model for every person. Such persons can be rewarded handsomely

3. Creation of ambassadors of good character in the same mould as goodwill ambassadors of sport. Such persons bring to mind the issue of character and how desirable a good character is for the well being of a nation.

4. Teaching of civics in schools should be encouraged so that from a tender impressionable age, children will be told the value of good character.

5. Failing families that cannot provide adequate parenting care should be identified and counseled. If need be they can be made to attend parenting classes to acquire necessary skills in this area. 6.Religious institutions should be seen as allies and encouraged to focus on character building programmes that will support what children get at home. Pre-marriage courses should be made compulsory so that only those who are prepared for marriage and raising children can be encouraged to do so. Ongoing marriage seminars should be encouraged for married persons on a regular basis.

7. Government should provide employment for youths. Long term youth unemployment erodes not only skills but also confidence, discipline and general social engagement. When youth with borderline character are not gainfully employed, criminal activities seem attractive to them.

8. Government should look at the prevailing social liberalism which has

resulted in the loosening of laws on divorce, abortion and contraception and take measures to mitigate the effect of these on character development of the young.

9. Fathering classes designed to equip men who need such skills will go a long way in helping fathers train their children properly.

SOME CHARACTER BUILDING THOUGHTS FOR YOUTHS

1. The following statements can be food for thought for your children to make them focus on certain aspects of their character with the goal of improving themselves.

2. "As a man thinks in his heart, so he is" [Proverb 23:7]. My thought life determines my actions which in turn form my habits that crystallize into character. In what ways can I reorder my thought life to enable me develop a good character?

3. Bad company corrupts good morals. Which of my friends share the same character goals with me? How can we be better partners in our character building goals?

4. I need self-disciplines in some areas of my life for my character to be transformed. In what aspects of my life do I urgently need attention?

5. I try to understand how some of my friends are feeling so I can be of help to them.

6. To err is human but to forgive is divine. I will want to be more forgiving in my relationships, making allowance for the shortcomings of others.

7. I believe in honesty. I tell the truth at all times and this will help me develop a personal culture of truthfulness. I distance myself from persons who lie with ease.

8. I say no to things that can corrupt my morals such as pornography and gambling. I will rather use my spare time in acquiring knowledge and skills.

9. I will say no to social habits like smoking and drinking which can gain control over my person by way of addiction.

10. Good performance in my studies will guarantee good opportunities in the job market. I will give my studies the attention it deserves to ensure upward social mobility for me.

11. Good character accentuates greatness. For this reason, I will pay the needed prize to develop a character that will withstand all challenges.

IN A NUTSHELL

1. Character is a vital resource in constructing a successful life; the foundations of good character are laid at home in the early years of life.

2. A two parent home is the most ideal environment for the development of good character. Consistent parental love and discipline blend to produce good character.

3. Social liberalism epitomized by high divorce rates, legalized abortions and contraceptive culture impact negatively on character development of children.

4. Parental classes organized for failing parents have been scientifically proven to be helpful in teaching parents the act of parenting. 5. Youth unemployment impacts negatively on character development because unemployed youths are quite often willing accomplices in criminal activities.

6. Government, schools and churches should have character education programmes to add on to what youths get at home.

LIFE APPLICATION

1. See yourself as uniquely positioned to shape the destiny of your child by helping him develop a good character. Take an inventory of the strength and weaknesses of your child and come up with measures to help him achieve his character goals.

2. Spend quality time with your child. Find out from him problem areas in his character growth and help provide the needed solutions.

3. Make out time to attend a parenting class or seminar at least annually. This will give you an opportunity to interact with other parents and also find answers to puzzling questions on parenting.

4. What are the greatest challenges to good character development in this age and how can fathers protect their children from these challenges?

5. What are the activities that provide mental toughness in children that can prepare them for life's tough challenges?

FURTHER READING

Richard Reeves; A Question of Character: *Prospect magazine* 149, August 2008

Successful Living in 2008-Advice from Benjamin Franklin; National Center for Constitutional Studies http://www.nccs.net/newsletter/jan08nl.html

Theodore Roosevelt; Character & Success; *The Outlook,* March 31, 1900 [http://www.foundationsmag.com/tr-character.html]

CHAPTER SIXTEEN
The Power of Commitment

FOCUSING QUESTIONS

1. *What is commitment?*
2. *Why is commitment important?*
3. *In which areas of life do children need commitment?*
4. *How can a Father help his children develop this value?*

WHAT IS COMMITMENT?

Commitment is giving your time, energy and other resources to a cause; it is an outward sign of your belief in a cause. Commitment is faithfulness in doing what you believe in whether convenient or not. It is at the heart of the purpose driven life. While children are often bored having to do the same thing on a daily basis, a Father's explanation that commitment is the price people pay for success may assuage them. Commitment is the power that births a dream; it sustains a person in the interregnum between a dream and the actual realization of the dream. Commitment is important in today's world of instant fix. Fathers have a responsibility of letting their wards know that nothing worthwhile is ever achieved without a prize. Children are taught commitment as they are given age-appropriate responsibilities, supervised and evaluated on their performance.

"Guard your spare moments well. They are like uncut diamonds. Discard them and their value will never be known. Improve them and they will become the brightest gems in a useful life."
Ralph Waldo Emerson

WHY IS COMMITMENT IMPORTANT?

Commitment is what ignites action in every project. It is the ultimate proof that you believe in what you are doing. Commitment is all about doing. There is a popular aphorism about commitment that says "When you hear something, you may forget it; when you see something, you may remember it but when you do something, you understand it". There is an old saying that says, *"Stand for something or you'll fall for anything"*. *Commitment is needed in the acquisition of knowledge, in maintaining relationships, in walking with God, in living a value-based life and in rendering public service.* **Commitment is defined by the following:**

Passion: This is a strong, compelling emotion about the task at hand that makes you want to see the desired end result.

Vision: This is having a mental image of the finished product. It is the act of seeing what others are not seeing.

A sense of mission: This makes you feel you have all it takes to realize your dream.

Focus: This entails setting your mind on the task at hand to the exclusion of all other things competing for attention.

Self-discipline-This means regulating your activities in such a way that all the resources [time, money, human resources etc] needed to achieve your goal are provided.

CHILDREN NEED COMMITMENT IN THE FOLLWING AREAS OF LIFE:

A **Commitment to Relationships**

Man is a social being; he does not exist as an island; that is why he is born into a family. Our lives are intertwined with those of others, either at home, school, church or in the neighbourhood. We are never alone; the extent to which we are able to relate to others amicably is the extent to which we will be loved and appreciated.

Stanford Research institute found that the money you make in any endeavour is determined only 12.5 percent by knowledge and 87.5 percent by your ability to deal with people. Former US president Theodore Roosevelt said, "The important single ingredient to the formula of success is knowing how to get along with people". **Relationship with God**

It is God's plan for children to learn about Him from their parents early in life. Fathers should capitalize on family devotions period to demonstrate what it is to have a relationship with God. Your children observe you to see how real God is in your life. Making bible reading a part of the family devotion provides knowledge of God to your children. When a father instructs his children on the right path to follow in life, because they have watched their Dad live out his faith, they may follow in his footsteps. **Relationship with Parents** A child should love and appreciate his parents; obedience to parents is an evidence of this love. Children should be committed to obeying their parents. Willful disobedience should always be sanctioned because it sends the wrong signal to other children; that they can do wrong and get away with it. A child that does not obey his parents that he sees cannot obey God that is invisible. In 1Samuel 2:22-36, we read of how the sons of Eli sinned persistently against God because they rejected the admonition of their father who asked them to desist from their evil ways. Eventually, they were judged by God and met their doom.

How can you instill obedience in to your children? When your child obeys a specific instruction, praise her; when she disobeys you, reprimand her. When children see that their parents insist on obedience, they live up to expectation. You must bear in mind that it is always difficult initially for children to see things from your perspective; however with the benefit of maturity and hindsight they will appreciate you for your role in their lives. A father can play dual roles in the lives of his children; he can be a wonderful father to one child and a deadly Dad to another. An example is David who properly tutored Solomon that later wrote the books of proverbs and Ecclesiastes but was a deadly Dad to his son Adonijah, which the bible said he never so much as scolded one day. A child that is used to obeying his parents will not find it difficult obeying authority figures in school and in society. This will keep such a child from being opposed to the law thereby giving the parents peace of mind.

How do children show respect and love for their parents? They do this as they greet their parents on waking up in the morning or when they get home from work. The highest expression of respect and love for parents is shown when children obey the instructions of their parents and turn out well in life. This brings honour to them and gives them the feeling that their efforts were not in vain. Children also show respect and appreciation when they remember the birthdays and wedding anniversaries of their parents by sending them cards or special greetings. They could also express themselves by buying gifts for their parents.

Relationship with siblings A father builds a healthy relationship among his children by:

1. Promoting love and respect among his children; he discourages name calling and self-depreciating jokes.

2. Children are made to eat together as a sign of unity.

3. The older children care for the younger ones especially when the parents are away from home.

4. The younger children defer to the older out of respect.

5. By acknowledging any special talent in each child and making the children feel special for their unique contribution to the family. This would prevent sibling rivalry.

6. If any child wins an award at school, that child is celebrated by all the family members.

7. If a child is sick and has to be on hospital admission, the children that are old enough can take their turns in providing company to the sick child.

Relationship with Friends A father encourages his children to have friends in the following ways:

1. Asking his children to be friendly and courteous to their mates.

2. Asking his children to bring their friends home so that he can interact with them.

3. He observes his children play and explains what it means to give and take in any relationship.

4. He encourages his children to share their toys with their friends.

5. He mediates in disagreements between his children and their friends and teaches them how to forgive when someone wrongs them.

6. He teaches them empathy by telling them to put themselves in their friend's position and experience their friend's feelings.

7. He teaches his children how to appreciate their friends by making them give birthday gifts or attend birthday parties, make birthday calls or spend time together.

8. When a friend is ill, a father can encourage his child to make a phone call or offer to assist in copying notes for the friend.

9   Keeping in touch either by visits or through phone calls.

Relationship with extended family members A father can present extended family members in a light that promotes a relationship with the aunties and uncles of his children. He can do this by

1. Making his children call their uncles, aunties, cousins, nieces and nephews on their birthdays and anniversaries.

2. Making them pay visits or go on holidays in their homes.

3. Keeping in touch through calls or electronic mails.

"What ever you can do or dream, you can, begin it. Boldness has genius, power and magic in it."
William H Murray

B Commitment to learning

Acquiring learning skills is a necessity for survival in the information age. It has been said that more than eighty percent of all scientists that ever lived are alive today. An estimated seventy percent of the medicines in use today were developed after World War II. Over fifteen thousand scientific journals are being published today, some with worldwide circulations. There is a deluge of information which can be utilized to realize one's goal in life.

How a Father Can Increase His Children's Commitment Learning?

You would do this in the following ways:

Read to your children By reading to your children when they are babies and making

them read books as they are growing up, you will be developing a reading culture in them. Teach them how to use the dictionary and how to expand their vocabulary. Ensure that every child of yours can read, write and do arithmetic.

Help them develop a right Attitude to learning Do all you can to make learning exciting and worthwhile to your children. Learning is crucial to meaningful existence in our present age. You need to make your children know that learning adds spice to life by exposing them to new findings from different scientific studies especially those relevant to successful living. **Ensure that your children do their homework always** Children feel home work is a drudgery and may not connect faithfulness in doing home work to improvement in academic ability.

Limit the number of hours your children spend watching the television while monitoring what they watch. TV is a universally known time waster. A summer 1999 study found African-American families have their TVs on for 76 hours per week [10.5 hours per day] according to Nielsen Research Media and TN Media; Latino families 60 hours, White/Asian Families for 40 to 50 hours per week. National Assessment of Education Progress tests of the US found that 34 percent of the poor readers watched six hours or more of TV a day as against 6 percent of the best readers.

Get your children involved in co-curricular and extracurricular activities These activities not only educate but build life skills into your children. Boys scout, Girls guild, Debating society, Christian

Fellowships are examples of groups that can add value to the lives of your children.

Ensure they develop good study habits. Since a pupil's academic workload increases with age, a child that has not developed effective reading habit will be seriously disadvantaged and return poor scores.

Increase your child's capacity to study. Progressively, ensure the length of hours spent reading increases as his academic workload increases. A daily time log of the hours spent reading can be kept as an objective proof of the child's efforts.

Let mastery of a subject be the goal of studying Let your children know that understanding a topic is important but gaining mastery over a topic is superior and should be the goal.

Further reading Tell your children it pays to read beyond what you are taught, it boosts your knowledge of the subject as well as raises your self-confidence.

Abhorrence for cheating Tell your children that cheating is morally wrong. It is an admission of failure in life which sets you up for further criminal activities in life. If you are caught, it will permanently dent your reputation.

Peer Learning Tell your children never to be ashamed of meeting their classmates who know a topic better than them for clarifications on any subject. It does not take anything away from a student when his peer explains things to him. **Setting academic goals** Teach your children how to set and attain academic goals. For instance, at the beginning of a new term or semester, your child can aim at getting As in a certain number of subjects. This would imply more work and less play. If

the child achieves his/her goals, it would boost his/her academic confidence. **Teach your children how to defer pleasure for a more appropriate time.** In his book, The Challenge of Affluence: Self-Control and Well Being in the United States and Britain since 1950[OUP], Avner Offer, Professor of economic history at Oxford proffers a picture of this challenge: "A young student ponders whether to spend the evening revising at her desk or to go out with her friends. Better marks mean better prospects, but dancing and drink are attractive too. Is it too much to sacrifice tonight for a remote future?" Let your children know your academic expectation of them; constantly raise the bar of your expectation. A 3-year study of 20,000 California and Wisconsin High School Students published in Beyond the Classroom by Dr Laurence Steinberg revealed the following:

Most American students don't take school seriously. They prefer to do a minimum just enough to get by to receive their diploma. Further earnings consequences for this low performance are not immediately clear to students. Academically bright students are often mocked by their peers as being psychological stress victims; in case of black students they are taunted of acting white A strong correlation was found between parents' expectation and general level of student achievement with a few exceptions. African-American and Latino parents are satisfied with any grades above D and their wards get mostly Cs. White parents are satisfied with grades above C and their children get mostly Bs. Asian parents accept A and their children bring mostly As."

Handling academic challenges and failures Tell your child that genius according to Thomas Edison is "One percent inspiration and ninety nine percent perspiration". Failure in an examination is just a proof that your preparation was not adequate; when you give an examination all it deserves, you are bound to excel. Your child may need extra lessons in some subjects or be peer-assisted to get mastery of his subjects.

C. Commitment to Value-Driven Life

Values are prized attitudes or strong moral benchmarks which have lasting advantage and worth to humanity; they safeguard society. A value-driven life is marked by good character, integrity, honesty, courage, justice, patience, delayed gratification, equity, fair play, industry, faithfulness, temperance, humility and modesty. Values are developed over a period of consistently living out your conviction in private and in public till it becomes deeply ingrained in you. Benjamin Franklin, one of the founding fathers of America, developed a personal programme which he called "the bold and arduous project of arriving at moral perfection". He listed thirteen virtues he desired to cultivate to arrive at his goal. The virtues were temperance, silence, order, resolution, frugality, industry, sincerity, justice, moderation, cleanliness, tranquility, chastity and humility. His plan was to focus on one virtue at a time and gain mastery over it before proceeding to the next.

As a father, you can discern the value needs of your children, discuss them with your children and have a plan of action to enable them acquire the values they need. You can enlist them in clubs or societies that can transmit these values into their lives. Be an example of these values to your children and use every opportunity to make your children practice them.

D. Commitment to Service

Service is an avenue of making children know that a life of consequence is one that is grounded in service to others; it is a life style to be embraced. Teach your children that service to humanity is a shortcut to greatness. Service elevates a man. The measure of a successful life is what a person gives back to society. No man gains recognition for what he received rather it is what you give that brings recognition to you. President Obama is an example of someone who rode on the back of public service to the United States White House. President Obama believed that service has a transformative power; helping both the individual that serves and the community that benefits. His love for service and willingness to serve as demonstrated in his antecedents were incontrovertible and these delivered crucial votes to him at the presidential polls of 2008. Let your children know that education is highly subsidized by Government; service is a means of giving back to society. Another positive effect of service is that it helps a child overcome the self-indulgent focus which is common among today's youth. Send your children to schools that integrate work and service into their regular curriculum. This will make service a part of their lives. As a father, encourage your children to be involved in any kind of public service that will add value to their live. Let them join clubs or societies that are involved in public service, it will help change their attitude and behaviour towards service. Pastor Arthur W. Rich in a baccalaureate sermon related this experience of his friend Bill. Bill belonged to a service club whose motto was "Service above self". One day, the President of the club asked if he could help an under privileged child who needs surgery to a hospital, 50 miles away. Bill obliged and this dialogue ensued as he drove Jimmy to the hospital. Jimmy looked toward Bill and said, "Mister, are you God"? "Oh, no", said Bill, "I'm not God, why do you ask"? Said the boy, "Last night, when I said my prayers, my mummy kissed me good bye and said that God would see that I got to the hospital, and that God would see that my legs are straightened so that I could run and play like other kids. You must be God". Bill reached over, patted his shoulder and said, "I'll accept that Jimmy, I guess you could say that I am working with God. And after getting to know you, I want to be a better worker for God in future". Then Jimmy's face lit up as he said, "Golly, Mister, God must be an awfully good Boss to work for". Arthur W. Rich DD, Pastor of First Baptist Church Lakeland, Florida. Baccalaureate Sermon delivered to the graduating class of 1968 at Lakeland Senior High school on June 2, 1968

IN A NUTSHELL

1. Commitment is giving all you have to a cause. It is the ultimate proof that you believe in what you are doing. Nobody ever achieved anything worthwhile without total commitment to the project.

2. Children can and should be taught commitment especially as it relates to relationships, learning, purpose-driven life and public service.

LIFE APPLICATION

1. How would you model commitment to your child on a day to day basis?

2. How would you explain the difference between interest in a cause and commitment to a cause to your teenage son?

FURTHER READING

Robert H Schuller: *Tough Times Never Last But Tough People Do* Laurence Steinberg: *Beyond the Classroom*

Jill Koenig: *The Power of Commitment; American Chronicle*

PART FIVE:
COMMUNICATION SKILLS, SOCIAL SKILLS, AND SELF-DEVELOPMENT SKILLS

"People are always blaming their circumstances for what they are. I don't believe in circumstances. The people who get on in this world are the people who get up and look for the circumstances they want, and, if they can't find them, make them."

George Bernard Shaw

CHAPTER SEVENTEEN

Communicating with Your Child

FOCUSING QUESTIONS

1. *Why is communication important?*

2. *What are the goals of communicating with your child?*

3. *How do you communicate with your child?*

4. *How do you develop good listening skills while talking with your child?*

THE IMPORTANCE OF COMMUNICATING WITH YOUR CHILD

Communication is the lubricant that oils your relationship with your child; it is an exchange of verbal and non-verbal information between you and your child. Through it your child gets to know how you feel about him and he too is able to reveal his thoughts, feelings and challenges to you. It is while speaking to him that you encourage him in his goals and pursuit while at the same time correcting him on his mistaken notions about life. Controlling methods used in communicating with your child in his childhood days are inadequate to deal with core moral issues that confront teenagers such as premarital sex, drugs, and pornography and examination malpractices. These require good communication skills on your part to make your child willing to discuss such issues with you.

When should a father start talking with his children? Researchers on early brain development had found that communicating with your child very early in life contributes to the child's growth and development. At eight years when a child would have started seeing and hearing about a wide array of topical and disturbing issues on the television such as sex, drugs, abortion, violence, and HIV/AIDs; it becomes necessary to talk to him on such issues. If you don't talk to him early, he will get inaccurate information on these issues from sources that do not share your moral convictions on these issues. You remain the first port of call for information on such issues during the preteen years of a child. When children get to the teenage years, they tend to depend more on their friends, media and outsiders for needed information. Talk to your child while he is young before others get to confuse him with information that goes against the values that you are instilling in him. **"The heart of a fool is in his mouth but the mouth of a wise man is in his heart. "**Benjamin Franklin

THE GOALS OF COMMUNICATING WITH YOUR CHILD

Let the following be your goals when communicating with your child:

Share what is in your mind If you are bothered about the kind of company your child keeps. Let your child know; he may discontinue the relationship.

Know what is in his mind If your child is bothered about anything, let him/her open up to you; your child should know that he/she has your ears.

Education You are one of his principal sources of education while he is growing up. Talk about challenges he would encounter while passing through different phases of life.

Respect for the differences in other people Different persons have different beliefs based on their convictions. It is good to respect people who hold differing views from you; it is the basis for harmony in a pluralistic society.

Guidance Provide guidance to your child on which path to follow in life. Counsel him whenever he is facing challenges in his education or behaviour.

Prepare him for the future This should not be left for when a father is terminally ill or is due to be away for a long period of time; it should be a regular thing for your child. Let him know that the future belongs to those who prepare themselves educationally as well in possessing life skills.

Correct your children A father who fails to correct his children has cheated them. Children need their father's admonition regularly to avoid such deadly traps like dishonesty, pornography, premarital sex and teenage pregnancy. **Teaching** Teach your child what good behaviour is as well as skills he needs to succeed in life. Teach him about ethics and morality; do not leave him for boarding schools or the Sunday school to teach. **Motivate your child to success** Children love to hear their Father say to them; "Daughter you have all it takes to do it". Children often rise to the challenge of meeting their father's expectation. Motivation will boost the confidence of your child. **Discipline** To discipline your child is to let him/her know that certain actions are inappropriate and have consequences. An undisciplined life has consequences for the child, parents and society at large. **Comfort him** If your child is hurting from disappointments of one kind or the other, comforting words from you would soothe him. Your child will one day reciprocate this gesture at your moment of need. **Praise** This is one need that children never have enough of; it increases their level of self acceptance.

"In order to succeed, you must know what you are doing, like what you are doing and believe in what you are doing."

Will Rogers

BEST PRACTICES IN FATHER-CHILD COMMUNICATION

Listen carefully to your child This is the only way to hear what he is saying or not saying.

Maintain eye contact with him This would enable you to observe any non-verbal communication which his body language may reveal.

Keep an open non-judgmental mind When your child knows that your mind is made up on some issues, he may not want to tell you what's in his mind.

Make sure your child understands what you are talking about Come to the level of your child when talking to him. Do not use words or phrases that are above his level. Get a feedback from him to be sure he is following the discussion.

Use open ended questions or ask his opinion on certain issues Opening sentences such as "What do you like about your new school" would allow your child to talk extensively about her school compared to a sentence like "How is your new school" to which your child may give the monosyllabic response of " Fine".

Listen to your child's response This will encourage him to talk since he knows you are listening. **Use reflective reasoning when necessary** On serious issues, reframe what your child has just said to be sure you got it right. This is the most effective way of communicating with your child because it confirms that you understood him/her. Recognize, respect and acknowledge your child's views which may be different from yours; try to discern the emotions behind your child's views by saying something like "You must have been disappointed by the way your teacher handled the issue".

Give your reaction This could be in the form of acknowledging your child's views and concerns and promising to do something over the issue. You can allay your child's fears by making statements like. "I will be at your school tomorrow morning to sort this issue out with your teacher".

Mind your choice of words Be mindful of your choice words so as not to give offense to your child. Choose to use words that empower, inspire, encourage and motivate when talking to your child. When you use curse or swear words such as "I know you will never make it in life", "You are a

let down of all my children"; such words will be deeply etched in the memory of your child such that long after you have forgotten that you uttered them, they keep haunting your child. Stock your child's memories with words like, "I know you are an outstanding child", "I am always proud of you, not even the sky can be your limit, daughter". Such words will not only boost your child's ego but will spur the child to further pursuit of excellence.

Be generous with compliments Be lavish with compliments; children thrive on it in building their self esteem. Words like very good, great. excellent, fantastic must not be depleted in your lexicon; they give life to your children.

Demonstrate affection Action speaks louder than voice is a truism; hugging your child without uttering a word conveys love and acceptance to the child. You can never do it too often. When your child is down cast from poor academic performance, use expressions like, "This is a temporary set back; I know this score does not reflect your ability on the subject. I believe when you give the subject the attention it deserves, you will come out with flying colours".

When you are away from home Stay connected with him by telephone, text messages or electronic mails. Call him from work if at the time of your getting home he would have gone to bed. **Write poems or compose songs** Highlight your child's special attributes by writing poems or songs that talk about his special talents. This communicates your impression about his talents to him in an unmistakable way.

Speaking the positive into existence This means calling into existence in your child those attributes that you desire in him that are presently lacking. This is based on the scriptural principal that God used when though Abram was childless, he changed his name to be Abraham which meant "Father of many nations". Abraham was to be the progenitor of the nation of Israel. You can decree good things into the life of your child in the same way. Also, you can make him change his negative utterances about his ability in this way; instead of saying "My physics is poor", he should say "I am improving in my physics". This creates an "I can do mentality in your child".

Apologize if an occasion calls for it When you fall short of your child's expectation apologize to him after admitting your failing. In this way you are teaching him to own up when he does anything wrong; you are also telling him in a tangible way that no one is above mistakes.

Tell him of your expectations. At every phase of his life, let him know what you expect of him; it helps to keep him focused.

Stay in touch with your child when he is away from home. Visit him at school if he is in the boarding house; ask him about the challenges he is facing and offer him encouraging words. Hand-delivered letters, emails and phone calls are the other ways you can stay in touch with your child.

When you have cause to disagree Do so with grace and dignity so that her self-respect is preserved. Let her know that until she matures, there are some decisions you will take on her behalf to protect her best interest.

Diversity of views and opinions There are as many views on different issues as there are people; educate your child that people's culture, upbringing, religious persuasion and education determine the view a person holds on a subject. It is impossible for a person to live his life to please another person. **When the timing is inappropriate** If you are very busy when your child needs your attention, say to him, "Son, right now I am very busy, come back in one hour's time when I will have all the time to discuss the issue with you". Do not shun your child off by saying "Can't you see that I am very busy"? **Growing need for privacy** Preteens experience a growing need for privacy as they approach the teenage years. Respect this need because your child needs space to discover himself. He may demand for more independence and may not be willing to divulge all that is going on in his life. Allow him reveal only what he wishes to reveal at this period of his life.

Try to be honest On issues you do not have clues to the answer, tell your child you do not know the answer. This will strengthen his/her ability to trust you and others. You may not go into all the details in answering a question, however do not leave too many blanks that a child may feel compelled to fill. **Review some family rules and upgrade his privileges** This may arise if he compares himself with his peers who are of similar background that enjoy greater privileges. This could be a demand for an increase in pocket money or time spent on watching TV or access to the internet.

Use everyday opportunities to talk Formal talk sessions with children always seem like classroom lectures which do not appeal to children; however seizing opportunities that might arise in course of the day to talk about tough issues will make a child more receptive to what you have to say.

Talk about it again and again You need to say the same thing over and over to a child before it clicks. Children's understanding is limited by age and inability to connect information to real life situations. Always ask for a recap of the information you gave your child so that you can fill in any knowledge gap.

How You Can Develop Good Listening Skills While Talking with Your Child

It is your duty to always make your child know that he can talk about what is going on in his life at any time. Establish a good line of communication with your child in the preteen years before he enters the turbulence of the teenage years that bring up a lot of complex issues. Good listening skills facilitate communication with children. Listen to what your child is saying or not saying. If your child looks upset, don't ignore it, instead remark it.

Be patient in listening if it seems it is taking forever for your child to get out his story. Do not help him in filling the gaps in his/her narration. In this way, your child is able to think at his own pace while at the same having the feeling that you cared enough to listen to him. **Stop whatever you are doing to give your child undivided attention.** Choose a time of the day that is convenient for both of you to talk on sensitive issues such as hurt

feelings, smoking, drinking, sex, cultism, sex education etc.

Allow your child to talk without interruptions from you. Switch off your phone to show your concern over the matter on hand.

Show that you are following by giving prompts such as nodding, smiling or grimacing.

Let your child know that no subject is a taboo for discussion.

Do not interrupt her or turn your discussion into a lecture that ends with a stern warning.

Talking down on your child may make her not to open up to you. Secondly, your child goes away with the impression that she can never measure up in life.

Consequences of Poor Father-Child Communication

1. The following may arise when a father fails to communicate with his children as they are growing up:

2. There will be lack of intimacy; communication promotes closeness between father and child.

3. Weak emotional bonding that results from not having much in common.

4. Increase incidents of father-child conflicts due to lack of understanding between father and child.

5. Persistent problems in the family because father and child cannot agree on how best to solve besetting problems.

6. Behavioural problems in children due to alienation of the father from nurturing of his children.

7. There will be increase in peer influence in the life of the child because your influence is minimal in his life.

SUGGESTED ISSUES FOR DISCUSSION WITH YOUR CHILD

The following subject matters depending on the age of your child may afford you the opportunity to practice the communicative skills discussed in this chapter:

1. School

2. Moral Values

3. Faith in God

4. Challenges he is facing presently 5. Vision for life

6. Goals and aspirations for the immediate

7. Money

8. Skills he wishes to acquire

9. Inventory of his talents

10. Making friends

11. Losing friends

12. Social vices such as drugs, examination malpractice, premarital sex, pornography and gambling.

13. Politics

14. Habits

15. Academic excellence

16. Handling hurt feelings

17. Racism

18. Family life

19. Choosing a life partner

20. Which college to attend?

IN A NUTSHELL

1. Communication is the means by which you know what is going on in the mind of your child as well as revealing what is on your mind to your child.

2. Mind what you say to your child because it stands a good chance of being fulfilled in your lifetime. 3.Cultivate diction of positive words that will shape the life of your child.

LIFE APPLICATION

1. On what issues do you have divergent views with your children apart from fashion and contemporary music? How can you bridge the gap in these areas?

2. When was the last time you had a one on one discussion with your child?

FURTHER READING

Stephen D Green, *Keys To Effective Father-Child Communication*. Child Development Specialist, Texas Cooperative Extension, October 2000.

Bray, J. H. and Heatherington, E.M. [1993]. Families in Transition: Introduction and Overview. *Journal of Family Psychology*, 7, 3-8.

CHAPTER EIGHTEEN
Social Skills

FOCUSING QUESTIONS

1. *Why are social skills important?*

2. *What influence do parents have on their children's social skills?*

3. *How can you enhance your child's social skills?*

4. *What are the practical ways of improving interpersonal skills in teenagers?*

5   *What is Emotional Intelligence?*

THE IMPORTANCE OF SOCIAL SKILLS

Social skills are skills that enable a child play constructively as well as develop friendship with age-mates; they are required for socialization. It is the skill required for getting along with peers and is an important indicator of a child's social development. When this skill is poorly developed, the child becomes socially isolated and is deprived of the exciting experiences of playing with other children. Research by early childhood professionals has found that a child's peer relationships are important for the child's development and adjustment to school.

RESEARCH FINDINGS ON SOCIAL SKILLS IN PRESCHOOL CHILDREN [UNDER FIVE]

The following are some of the findings on social skill acquisition in children under five years of age:

1. Preschool age children [Under fives] who have positive peer relationships are likely to get along well with their mates in elementary school while children with poor relationship skills are likely to have problems relating to their mates in school. Children need acceptance by their mates to enjoy school and when this is lacking, they may have academic difficulties as a result of it.

2. Children with poor social skills are excluded from opportunities to develop additional and more complex skills important for future peer interactions [Eisenberg, Cameron, Tryon & Dodez 1981].

3. Children with good social skills who get on well with other children are found to have agreeable disposition. They also have additional skills that make play more exciting and fun; they are able to recognize other children's preferences, behaviour and interests and adapt to them accordingly.

4. Children with antagonistic behaviours who disrupt the play of their mates are disliked by their peers.

5. Children with good social skills are responsive and able to fit in with the behaviour of their play partner; this makes them acceptable.

6. Children with good social skills are quick at offering play alternatives to their mates; this enables them maintain longer play bouts without having quarrels with their mates.

"Any man can be a father, but it takes a special person to be a dad."

Anonymous

PARENTS' INFLUENCE ON THEIR CHILDREN'S SOCIAL DEVELOPMENT

The daily interaction between a father and his children can go a long way in helping his children develop social skills in their first six years of life. Parental responsiveness and nurturance are key factors in developing social skills in little children under five. Loving and responsive parenting help children see the world in a positive light and to expect relationship with others to be rewarding. A good parent-child relationship is marked by positive and agreeable interactions that make the child feel accepted. Such parents play very often with their children while they use physical punishment and coercive discipline minimally.

HOW YOU CAN ENHANCE YOUR CHILD'S SOCIAL SKILLS

1. Provide your child ample opportunities to play and interact with his age mates such as you have in birthday parties, day care, nursery school and Sunday school classes. The experiences he gains on such occasions become handy when he begins elementary school. Children who have had long term relationship with

their age mates have fewer relationship problems than children who have only had short term relationships. A long term relationship has the advantage of enabling the child develop more sophisticated social strategies.

2. Play with your child in a peer-like way for the fun of it. When you play with your child as if you are mates during play time, you impart more advanced social skills to your child that enables him/her get along better with peers.

Play with in an effective peer-like way and your child will yearn always for such interactions. During such plays, laugh and smile, respond to his play ideas while avoiding criticisms of his play styles or trying to take over the play initiative from him. Your play sessions should reflect equality in your interactions, do not dominate the play, strive to follow your child's ideas and have fun as equals. The effect of such plays with your child is that he feels good and confident as effective play partner and so he looks forward to playing with his mates. Secondly, this kind of play instills a positive outlook in him towards others that makes him look forward to play opportunities with people outside the family.

3. Observe your child while at play with his friends. Teach him to learn to share his toys with his visiting friends. This makes him generous and self-less when it comes to relating with his peers. When your child visits his friends and would like to take his friends' toys away at the end of play, you would tell him to return the toy since he has his toys at home. In this way, he gets to

know that individuals have their own possessions.

4. Talk about social relationship and values. Opportunities for such talks come either when you are taking him to school, on his way back from school or at meal times and other informal settings. Use events that happened at school for such conversations which aim to tell him the importance of friends and how to be friendly. Children measure the love you have for them through such occasions and are very receptive to ideas and skills you pass on to them at such informal periods.

5. Help your child solve some of the problems of his mates. If during a chat with your son, he tells you about one of his mates called Henry whom nobody wants to play with, a dialogue like this may ensue;

Dad: Why do you think nobody wants to play with Henry?

Son: He is a new student and he also stammers a lot?

Dad: In what way can you help him come out of his shell?

Son: I will go to him during break time and tell him my name and ask him to play with me.

Dad; That will be very nice of you; it will make Henry happy.

When you encourage your child to think in terms of the feelings and needs of his mates, it makes him more acceptable to his mates.

6. Encourage your child to use positive relationship strategies such as negotiation or compromise when there are differences between him and his friends rather fighting or employing verbal coercion [Using expressions like "I won't play with you again"]. You can do this by talking to your child.

7. Show him how to handle social setbacks or rejection. When your child's mate refuses to play with him, tell him to see this rejection as temporary; tell him that he can change the situation by being friendlier [Behaviour change]. As a father, make excuses for the child that rejected playing with your child instead of calling the child names. This makes your child have optimistic views, resilient attitude and belief that social situations can be improved with effort and positive behaviour.

8 Observe older children work out differences with their mates when possible. This helps them gain skills in resolving conflicts.

PRACTICAL WAYS OF IMPROVING INTERPERSONAL SKILLS IN TEENAGERS

Interpersonal skills are social skills you employ in dealing with people; they determine how others perceive you and how they respond to you. They are skills that promote good relationship among people through enhancing a person's capacity to understand the intentions, motivations and desires of other people. Teach and model the following behaviours to your teenage child:

Learn to smile People often respond with a smile when you smile to them. It conveys the impression that you are well disposed to communicate with the person.

Be respectful especially to persons in authority and those older than you. Respecting people portrays you as a well groomed person who can be trusted.

Learn to greet people even those you are meeting for the very first time This is another proof that you are a well groomed child.

Cultivate a civil diction Learn to use the word please when you are asking for a favour. You may ask for direction from a total stranger by saying "I am sorry to bother you, Sir, could you show me the way to the main market"?

Be friendly Always reach out to your friends and offer assistance when it is within your power to do so; then you will retain your friends. **Develop Empathy** Your ability to share in another person's emotional feelings or putting yourself in another person's situation makes you an understanding person whom others would love to be around. **Optimism** People who look at the brighter side of things are greater fun to be with than those who look at the dark side of things. Optimism can be developed by those who value it.

Be appreciative If you appreciate people rather than see them as rivals, people will stick around you. People who appreciate others do not have a critical spirit. **Good Listener** Listening attentively to people is a sign that you appreciate and value them; people will love to hang around you.

Be discrete This is the ability to keep what you were told in confidence. If you are disciplined enough to keep secret what you were told in confidence, people will trust and love your company.

Be unassuming Take people for who they are. Do not read meaning to their every action, and then they will feel safe to be with you. **Nurture a good sense of humour** See the lighter side of things; humour people but not at the expense of other persons. Learn to laugh heartily especially at yourself. **Be generous with compliments** If you pay compliments freely, everybody will like to be in your company; there are too many persons that are stingy with compliments. Compliments make people feel taller while unjust criticism diminishes people.

Be a peacemaker If you are a peace maker, you will attract decent people to your side who share your values. Help people resolve their conflicts instead of escalating it, they will appreciate you.

Pay attention to others People are drawn to persons, who care for others; who are never too busy to spare moments for their friends.

Be a clear communicator When you say what you mean and mean what you say, people take you seriously because they know where they stand with you.

Share knowledge with others Be willing to share knowledge with your peers who need your assistance. However, sharing knowledge during examination is wrong and should not be indulged in.

Be willing to lead Be willing to provide leadership for your peers especially in realizing your goals in learning.

Show team spirit When you are a good team player, your peers will like you.

Be a catalyst for change Be a positive influence among your peers, a rallying point for all that is good.

"The conduct of our lives is the true mirror of our doctrine."

Montaigne

EMOTIONAL INTELLIGENCE

Emotional Intelligence as defined by Goleman [1998] is the capacity for recognizing our own feelings and those of others, for motivating ourselves and for managing emotions well in us and in our relationships. It is a learned capability that can be nurtured to high levels. The competences that define emotional intelligence have been arranged in four groups [Boyatzis, Goleman & Rees 1998] - self-awareness, self-management, social awareness and social skills. Your children will grow in their emotional intelligence as they know themselves and others better in terms of feelings and emotions. **How can your child develop it?** Your child can develop it by knowing his/her emotions, strengths and weaknesses; by knowing the emotions of others and relating with them on the basis of this knowledge. **What is the value of emotional intelligence?**

It enables your child to monitor his own emotions as well as those of his mates so that he is able to relate with others on the basis of the information he has. An emotionally intelligent child would recognize that his friend is unhappy today and so would not bother him to come and play.

Emotional intelligence assists in creating mutual understanding when there is disagreement.

IN A NUTSHELL

1. Children need social skills to socialize and be accepted by their peers.

2. You can enhance their social skills in many different ways.

3. Emotional intelligence is an added advantage when dealing with people.

LIFE APPLICATION

What are the social skills that each of your children needs and how can you help him get the skills?

FURTHER READING

Dale Carnegie; *How to Win Friends and Influence People*

CHAPTER NINETEEN
Self-Development Skills

FOCUSING QUESTIONS

1. *What are self-development skills?*

2. *Why are they important?*

3 *How can your child acquire them?*

These are skills a person needs to improve his behaviour in such a way that the quality of his life is enhanced. The power for getting these skills lies in a person; however it has to be discovered, nurtured and released for daily living. The list of skills includes self esteem or self-concept, self confidence, and self-control.

SELF-CONCEPT OR SELF-ESTEEM

This is what a person thinks about him/ herself; it is the value a person puts on his/ her person. A person will evaluate him/ herself on physical appearance, moral values, personality type, family status, social skills and academic attainment. Your self-esteem is determined by what you think of yourself, what others think of you as well as the perception of the ways in which you are similar to or different from other persons in your class. People with good self-esteem are self-confident, bustle with life and enjoy living; they are easy to get along with. Persons with low self-esteem lack self-confidence, are easily confused and can take offense on little issues, they are difficult to relate with.

"Watch your thoughts; they become your words. Watch your words; they become your actions. Watch your actions; they become your habits. Watch your habits; they become your character. Watch your character; it becomes your destiny."

Anonymous

A FATHER'S ROLE IN THE DEVELOPMENT OF SELF-CONCEPT IN HIS CHILD

Good father-child relationship Make sure you communicate love, respect and acceptance to your child in your interactions. What your child thinks of himself derives from what he believes you think of him.

Play with your child and spend time with him because he quantifies your love for him by the amount of time you spend with him.

Affirm your children Verbally affirm your love for the person of your child and physically demonstrate affection for him/ her by hugging, holding hands, and kissing. Let your love be unconditional, celebrate achievements but do not let it be your condition for loving them.

Teach your child how to love himself
He can do this as he cares for his person by way of maintaining good personal hygiene, eating healthy foods, exercising and having good friends. He must learn to think positively about himself.

Identify and develop the talents he has
When a child gets recognized for a talent that his peers do not have, it boosts his self-esteem. If he has a talent for music, send him to music lessons or get a piano teacher for the child, when the child's skills improve, he will be proud of his achievement and his peers would hold him high.

Use encouraging words on your child
Expressions like "I know my son is up to the task" would make your son believe in himself.

Develop a good dress sense People tend to form good opinions about you from the manner of your dressing. If your dressing is appropriate for an occasion, people will think well of you.

Teach your child how to talk to himself positively An example of a positive self-talk is "Although I failed the English test, I will give English more attention and have a good score in the next test to make up for this failure. I refuse to be discouraged because I have all it takes to excel".

Mastery over academic tasks When your child through dint of hard work and not by cheating at tests and examination improves his grades, his feelings about himself will improve. His mates will also rate him high.

Give him household responsibilities
Handling household chores, cleaning the car, sweeping premises are duties that improve a child's sense of responsibility and self-worth.

Help him in developing good social skills When you have many friends as a teenager because of your good social skills, it is a sort of approval rating that you have qualities that many people like. This will make you feel good about your self.

Teach him how to make friends You make friends by being friendly; have good feelings for your mates, be empathetic when your mates are in difficulties and have a kind word for people.

Help him to love challenges When young persons do what their mates find difficult to do, they feel good about themselves while their mates rate them high.

Teach him how to handle failures Let him know that failing at a task does not make your person a failure, it only means you have got to try harder. Success in life is most often the outcome of many failed attempts.

Give your child opportunities to visit new places and learn new skills. This will make him feel good about himself because he has what his mates do not have.

Consequences Of Low Self-Concept

Unfulfilled life A child with low self-concept keeps wishing to be a person he is not and this drains enthusiasm from him.

Unstable ways A person with low self-esteem cannot be his own person because of always trying to live up to other people's expectations.

Feelings of insecurity A person with low self-esteem is afraid to reveal his true nature so that he will not suffer a rebuff from his peers. **Touchiness** Low self-esteem persons feel touchy because they feel people are picking on them. **Always looking for acceptance** They look for the love they did not get from their father in other men and so females with this problem get exploited sexually by unscrupulous men.

Prone to developing bad habits Persons with low self esteem often hide their insecurity by taking to alcohol, smoking, cultism and joining groups of deviant persons who give them a feeling of belonging.

Always ready to dominate or control others Persons with low self-esteem love to project themselves or gain recognition at the expense of others. This could make them unbearable during interaction.

SELF ASSESSMENT TESTS ON SELF-CONCEPT

1. Do I feel good about myself to the extent that I make friends easily and enjoy my relationships?

2. Do what I feel about myself depend on what others feel or say about me?

3. Do I consider myself a failure because I failed at a task?

4. Do I feel inferior to my mates?

5   Do I wish I look different?

6. On a scale of 0 to 10, how would I rate myself?

SELF-CONFIDENCE

This is your belief in your ability to perform a task successfully. It comes from self-knowledge of your strength and weaknesses. When your prediction of success in a given task comes to pass, it means your self-confidence is high. When you are uncertain about your performance in any examination, it means your self confidence is low. Your self-confidence can be low in one subject while it is high in another.

Your self-confidence increases as you succeed in different tasks you have undertaken.

HOW A FATHER CAN ENHANCE HIS CHILDREN'S SELF-CONFIDENCE

Help your child nurture good self-esteem When a child feels he is capable of performing a task successfully, his self-confidence rises.

Create the right environment at home; when you subject your child to a barrage of criticism, his self-confidence withers while praise and affirmation boosts self-confidence. **Help him gain mastery over the subject or acquire** skill in the subject by having extra lessons on it. When he does well at subsequent examination, his self-confidence in that subject will rise. When a child improves on his soccer skills, his confidence in his soccer ability will rise.

Positive Self-Talk A person who tells himself that he has all it takes to surmount his current challenges will do well compared to a person who is expecting a failure in his attempt.

Persistence Those who persist at overcoming an obstacle in life gain self-confidence when they succeed.

Setting achievable goals It could be frustrating and confidence draining when a child attempts the impossible. Let him start with small goals that are within his ability. Nothing boosts a child's self-confidence as much as success.

Handling failure Let your child know that failure is always an opportunity to learn more about a subject or task. It should not be turned into an exercise for self-denigration.

Envisioning success When you think and dream success coupled with paying your dues in terms of hard work, you will succeed and this will boost your confidence.

Move with self-confident persons When you keep the company of achievers, you get to learn their ways of doing things and this will translate into success for you.

"When we do the best we can, we never know what miracle is wrought in our life, or in the life of another."

Helen Keller

CONSEQUENCES OF LOW SELF-CONFIDENCE

Unfulfilled life People With low self-confidence are unable to muster what it takes to make success out of life.

Can easily be misled Unscrupulous persons exploit those with low self-confidence by making them do what is wrong.

Poor judgment This can arise from not knowing what is right from wrong.

The butt of jokes Peers who believe a person is "dumb" would make him the butt of jokes.

SELF-ASSESSMENT TESTS ON LEVEL OF SELF-CONFIDENCE

1. What are the subjects in which I have consistently scored high marks?

2. What are the subjects in which I have always scored low marks?

3. What tasks can I perform very well with very little stress?

4. Do I like answering questions in the class?

5. How do my classmates perceive me?

6. Am I a leader or follower among my peers?

7. On a scale of 0 to 10 how would I rate my self-confidence level?

SELF-CONTROL

Self-control can be defined as having control over your actions which may give you immediate and easy gratification. It demands recognizing and controlling passions, emotions, desires, wishes and choosing what is right. Children, teenagers and youth may act impulsively to satisfy a perceived need; self-control is the learned behaviour that puts a check on our actions. Self-control operates from a base of knowing what is right from what is wrong. Self-control protects a child from impulsive, insensitive and adventuresome actions which may land him/her in danger.

Children in Preschool and Elementary School age should be taught self-control in the following areas:

1. Anger control It is okay to be angry but wrong to hit or scream at someone when angry. When a situation is annoying or

provocative a child can be taught to walk away from it instead of fighting.

2. Play time comes after the school assignment or homework of a child has been done.

3. Time spent on TV is limited to children's programme.

4. Not to intrude when adults are talking.

5. Complying with bedtime rules.

6. Coping with denied requests.

7. Coping with feelings of sadness or frustrations.

Teenagers and Youths should develop self-control in the following areas of their lives:

Anger control Children watch a lot of violent films which invariable affect how they respond to this emotion. Fighting is a bad way of managing anger. Teach your children to learn to walk away from the scene of provocation; then relax and take some deep breaths and tell the person in a calm voice why you are angry.

Use of time The time lost is gone forever. Time waits for no one. Your child needs to be taught how to manage his/her time in order to achieve set goals.

Learning There is so much to learn in this phase of life. It requires self-control to sit down and acquire knowledge required for progress in life.

Money management Youths must have self-control over their use of money; they must learn the habit of staying within their budget.

Use of the tongue Self-control over the tongue is one of the indicators of maturity; it must be acquired in this phase of life.

Resisting social vices Youths need self-control to resist habits such as smoking, taking hard drugs, pornography, premarital sex, teenage pregnancy and alcoholism.

Being law abiding Keeping rules at home, school and society at large demand self-control on the path of youths.

Avoiding bad company It takes self-control to avoid bad company and follow those who share similar values with you.

Controlling time spent on TV and Internet These are established time-wasters that require good self-control measures to escape its trap.

SELF-ASSESSMENT TESTS ON LEVEL OF SELF-CONTROL

1. How do I react to provocation?
2. When last did I engage in any violent act?
3. How many hours do I spend watching TV or surfing the net?
4. Do I smoke, drink or use hard drugs?
5. Am I a spendthrift?
6. How do I control my sexual urges or passion?
7. On a scale of 0 to 10, how would I rate myself?

IN A NUTSHELL

1. Self-esteem or self-concept is the worth a person places on him/herself.

2. Self-confidence is the perceived ability of a person to successfully carry out a task.

3. Self-control is having control over your actions which may seem rewarding at face values but may have negative effects on your person on the long run.

LIFE APPLICATION

1. What strategies will you use to help your child who is always running foul of school laws?

2. In what areas of life do you model self-control to your children?

FURTHER READING

Clark. L. (1996). *SOS! Help for Parents* (2nd Edition). Parents Press Louise Eckman, *Self Control for Children*

Tom G Stevens, *You Can Choose To Be Happy*

PART SIX:
SELF-MANAGEMENT SKILLS

"Take your needle, my child, and work at your pattern; it will come out a rose by and by. Life is like that; one stitch at a time taken patiently and the pattern will come out all right, like embroidery."

Oliver Wendell Holmes

Chapter Twenty

Attitude Makes the Difference

Focusing Questions

1. *What is attitude?*

2. *Why is attitude important?*

3. *What are the determinants of a child's attitude?*

4. *What are the factors that influence a child's attitude?*

5. *What are the desirable attitudes that a teenager can adopt?*

6. *What are the undesirable attitudes a teenager should avoid?*

What Is Attitude?

Attitude is your manner of acting or behaviour that reveals how you feel deep within you. Very often attitude is expressed by body posture or verbally in a way that depicts a person's mood. When attitude is used as slang, it describes a sullen or quarrelsome disposition.

Why Is Attitude Important?

Your attitude at any point in time speaks loudly about your disposition to the person you are with or the task at hand. If you display a friendly attitude, the person you are with feels confident that you will serve his best interests. Attitude has been described as the mind's paint brush because it colours any and every situation.

"Your living is determined not so much by What life brings to you, As by the attitude you bring to life...Not so much by what happens to you, As by the way your mind looks at what happens. Circumstances and situations do colour life, But you have been given the mind to choose What the colour should be."

John Miller

This simple exercise says a lot about the place of attitude in how you manage your affairs. Attach numerical value to the 26 alphabets as below beginning from 1 to 26 with A being 1 and Z being 26

A B C D E F G H I J
K L M N O P Q R S T
V W X Y Z

Attach numerical values to the letters that spell Attitude and sum it up; what you get is 100.

A T T I T U D E
1 2O 20 9 20 21 4 5 ===== 100

K N O W L E D G E
11 14 15 23 12 5 4 7 5 ===== 96

C H A R A C T E R
3 8 1 18 1 3 20 5 18 ===== 77

What the above tells you is that attitude affects every facet of a person's life.

Attitude affects a child's physical health, mental health and ability to recover from an illness. A firm belief that you will recover from an illness often accelerates recovery.

Your attitude determines people's perception of you and how they interact with you. If you have the right attitude people will want to interact with you constructively. Attitude can become a self-fulfilling prophecy. If you go through life expecting success in your endeavours, you will get your heart's wish.

WHAT ARE THE DETERMINANTS OF A CHILD'S ATTITUDE?

The following are the interplay of factors that determine a child's attitude as he goes through different phases of life:

Early Life Environment Attitudes are developed early in life; right attitudes when instilled in a child stay with the child into adulthood. A loving, caring and positive home environment serves as catalyst in the development of right attitudes. It takes a lot of self determination to correct a wrong attitude once it is imbibed in early life. A child raised with affirmation at home grows to be a friendly person while the one raised with harsh criticism becomes a self-defensive, distrustful person. **Parental Influence** Parents that model caring for the poor and needy will have children who are kind hearted and willing to help people in need.

Life Experiences Some people who knew lack while growing up will choose to be generous when they succeed in life.

Self-Esteem A child with a good image of him does not feel threatened by the success of others. He believes his turn to shine is by the corner.

Self-Confidence A self-confident child does not run others down so that he will get attention.

Personal Value System A child with a good positive value system will always align with good causes.

Personality type Children with gregarious nature are friendlier and more outgoing than those with melancholic disposition. Children with melancholic disposition can be trained to be exciting persons.

The Training a child gets A child trained to look at the brighter side of life will continue in that attitude when he is grown.

A Child's choice of friends If you move with a pessimist long enough, you will only see the darker side of things.

Exposure to books, TV and The Internet A child is affected positively or negatively by the books he reads, the programmes he watches on the television as well as the internet.

School environment A child that attends a school that combines academics with moral education will have a positive disposition to life.

"A pessimist sees the difficulty in every opportunity; An optimist sees the opportunity in every difficulty."

Sir Winston Churchill

HINTS ON HOW TO HELP YOUR CHILD DEVELOP THE RIGHT ATTITUDES

From Ages 1 to 6

Let him experience acceptance from you as you play with him; he will learn to accept others and play with them too.

1. Teach him to greet using words like "Hello", "Good morning", "Bye"

2. Teach him how to say "Sorry" to a hurting person, how to say "I am sorry" and "Thank you".

3. Teach him how to smile heartily.

Ages 6-10

1. Teach your child how to have a positive image of himself.

2. He should learn to celebrate with friends by attending birthday parties of peers.

3 He should learn to pay compliments.

4. He should value punctuality.

5. He should not laugh at people. He should develop interest in co-curricular and extracurricular activities He should learn how to stay out of trouble at school and in the neighbourhood.

Ages 11 to 21

Learn to be a positive influence among age mates.

1. Develop goals in life and have a career in mind.

2. Choose to be happy in life even when things do not turn out as planned.

3. Learn to make and sustain friends. 4 Train your child to know that others can only stop him temporarily from attaining his goals in life; he alone can do so permanently.

5. Refuse to be limited in life by records set by other persons. World records are always broken; the 1936 Olympic swimming records were the qualifying entry time for the 1972 record. He can strive to be a record breaker. Words like "I can't" should be replaced by "I can"; "It's too hard" by "I can do it"; "I don't have the time" by "I will make the time" etc

6. Know that your choices have repercussions; therefore avoid delinquent behaviours.

7. Do not allow people to create your world for you, otherwise they would make it too small.

8. Avoid people who make you unhappy.

DESIRABLE ATTITUDES THAT TEENAGERS CAN ADOPT

The following attitudes will stand teenagers in good stead if adopted: **Attitude to time** Time must be maximized because it does not wait for any body. Time lost cannot be regained.

Attitude to punctuality Punctuality remains the soul of business while at the same time marking you out as a serious person. **Attitude to money** Money is not everything; it is a good servant but a bad master. It must be handled with care.

Attitude to life Life is always fair, it gives you what you deserve. As a man lays his bed so he lies on it.

Attitude to failure and setback That you failed at a task does not make you a failure;

it only means you need more wisdom and skill to get it right.

Attitude to opportunities Seize every opportunity that comes your way to learn of do good because you may not have it again.

Attitude to impression You only have one opportunity to create a first impression, so maximize it.

Attitude to learning Bear in mind that we are in an information age where life-long learning is the norm. The one who has knowledge will always be the boss of the person without knowledge.

Attitude to correction Accept correction gracefully because no one is above mistakes. We are also in a fast changing world where what is current today may be obsolete tomorrow. Do not live in the past.

Attitude to change The only constant thing in life is change; most mental illnesses arise from inability to adapt to change.

Attitude to giving Be generous in giving; people are remembered for what they gave and not what they received. 'Givers never lack' is an aphorism that has stood the test of time.

Attitude to elders Always respect elders because one day, you too would be old.

Attitude to constituted authority They are there to protect your interest; always align with them.

Attitude to rules and regulation You are a civilized person to the extent to which you obey rules and regulations.

Attitude to human life Uphold the sanctity of human life in every situation and protect it. To cheapen human life is to cheapen your own life.

Attitude to obligations and responsibilities Discharge your obligations and responsibilities well and you will be considered a responsible citizen.

Attitude to corrupt practices Shun corruption becomes it will ultimate destroy the lives of those who indulge in it. Whatsoever a man sows, that will he reap

Attitude to the less privileged Use your power to protect their interest at all times. Your attitude to the less privileged especially widows and orphans is a reflection of your character.

Attitude to public property Use it with care; it is a test of how civilized you are.

Attitude to taxes and bills Pay your taxes and bills as a responsible citizen.

Attitude to customers Remember you are in business because of their patronage, so treat them as kings.

Attitude to queuing It promotes orderliness and it portrays you to be a decent person.

Attitude to freedom Use your freedom wisely and purposefully.

Attitude to public funds It is given to you in trust, so use it judiciously and be accountable; demarcate your personal account from public treasury.

Attitude to commitments You are a responsible person if you fulfill your commitments at all times

Attitude to debts Debts are meant to be paid.

Attitude to fraud It is a reprehensible act which decent people have zero tolerance for.

Attitude to food You eat to live and not the other way round; eat rightly and in moderation to stay in good health.

Attitude to examination malpractices It is a despicable act which should not be tolerated.

Attitude to forgiveness To err is human but to forgive is divine; you are a noble person when you forgive or keep short accounts of wrongs done to you.

THE OPTIMIST CREED

To be just as enthusiastic about the success of others as you are about your own.

To forget the mistakes of the past and press on to the greater achievements of the future.

To wear a cheerful countenance at all times and give every living creature you meet a smile.

To give so much time to the improvement of your self that you have no time to criticize others.

To be too large for worry, too noble for anger, too strong for fear and too happy to permit the presence of trouble.

Optimist International

IN A NUTSHELL

1. Attitude is your manner of behaviour that reveals how you feel deep within you. It colours every action of yours.

2. A host of modifiable factors determine the attitude of a person. A child's attitude can be modified for the better by the father very early in life.

3. There are desirable and undesirable attitudes; every child is at liberty to choose the kind of attitude that fits his lifestyle.

LIFE APPLICATION

1. What attitude would you want to model for your child?

2. What are the wrong attitudes in your life that you would not want your child to adopt?

FURTHER READING

John Maxwell: *The Winning Attitude*

Patrick R Gruber, M.S., Shirley C Eagan, Ed .D *The Winning Attitude.* West Virginia University Extension Service

CHAPTER TWENTY-ONE
Money Management Skills

FOCUSING QUESTIONS

1. *Why is money important?*
2. *What are the basic monetary concepts you need to teach your children about?*
3. *How can you help your children develop their opinion about money?*
4. *How to teach your children money management skill*

THE IMPORTANCE OF MONEY

Money was aptly described in Wall street Journal as an *"article which may be used as a universal passport to everywhere except heaven and as a universal provider of everything except happiness"*.

To deny the importance of money is to live in self-deceit; however the following facts must be taught our children about money:

Money can be a great blessing or a terrible curse. It is a great blessing when used to meet our needs and that of others or a terrible curse when it has paralyzing grip over you such that you cannot use it for the good of others.

Money would want to be your God if you allow it. It does this by giving you a false sense of security and making you want to get it at all costs. Some persons can do anything for money, like kill, maim or cheat because they see money as an end in itself.

Money talks depending on the language you want it to speak. It can make you boast and feel on top of the world while it can speak the language of charity when used to help the poor and the needy.

"Dug from the mountain side or washed in the glen Servant am I or master of men. Earn me, I bless you: Steal me, I curse you Grasp me and hold me, A fiend shall possess you. Lie for me, die for me, Covet me, take me Angel or devil, I'm just what you make me."

Author Unknown

Money does not grow on trees. If you do not have control over how you spend it, you will always be in need of it.

Money can develop wings; therefore use it wisely when it is in your custody. In 1923, a group of 7 men whose combined wealth was greater than that of the US treasury gathered for a meeting at the Edgewater Beach Hotel in Chicago; they epitomized success and prosperity. Twenty five years later, their lot had changed. Charles Schwab, president of the largest steel company had died penniless; Arthur Cutten, millionaire wheat speculator had died penniless. Richard Whitney of the New York Stock Exchange had spent years in prison, Albert Fall; a member of the presidential cabinet had been released from prison so he could die at home. Jesse Livermore, Leon Fraser and Ivan Krueger had taken their lives.

It is what we give that makes us rich not what we grab. It was Henry Ford who said, "Money is just like an arm or a leg-you either use it or lose it".

BASIC MONEY CONCEPTS YOU NEED TO TEACH YOUR CHILD.

Your child needs to know about earning, spending, saving, borrowing and giving as early in life as is feasible. He gets to know about earning when he is given monetary gifts; he gets to know about spending when he buys things with his money while he gets to know about saving when he keeps his money with you in his safe. Children need the maturity of early teenage years to understand borrowing and giving.

Earning is a reward and recognition for your services; it has a relationship with your job, time, skills and energy. If your son is old enough to distribute newspaper for an earning, help him set up an earnings record book to record his expenses against his earnings with a goal of finding the break-even point.

Spending is an easier task than earning. It requires more self-discipline to control spending; you must differentiate between your wants and your needs while living within your means. Keep records of your spending and be accountable for the decisions you make. The overhead that goes with certain financial decisions should be spelt out to children.

Saving means having your mind for the future or planning to buy something for which you do not presently have the money. It entails delaying gratification to achieve an end. Saving can be made a regular habit. You can save your money in the bank for which you earn an interest or save it at home.

Borrowing means asking for somebody else's money to use for a time with a promise to pay back. When you borrow from a bank, you pay an interest on what you borrow. Buying now and paying later is a form of borrowing for which you pay a higher rate. Borrowing for your wants is foolhardy while borrowing to further your education is commendable.

Giving is sharing what you have for a noble cause such as helping a person in need. Do not wait till you have a lot of money before you start giving. You are under obligation to pay your taxes and bills.

"It's not what you'd do with a million If riches should be your lot It's what you are doing at present With the dollar and quarter you've got."

Unknown

HOW TO HELP YOUR CHILD DEVELOP HIS OWN POLICY ABOUT MONEY

It is a good practice to talk about your feelings and opinions about money to your child's hearing; it exposes him to your policy about money. A father is in a unique position to help his child differentiate between self-worth and net worth. Self-worth is the value you put on yourself and it is not affected by the amount of money in your account. Your net worth is the amount of wealth you have accumulated over the years as reflected in your bank account and assets. A person should be judged by his self-worth, his contribution to society and not by how much he is worth financially.

Tell your child that determinants of financial success include intelligence, academic attainment, professional career, talent, hard work, intuition, timing and luck. While teaching your child about money, create an emotional and intellectual climate that would help him learn to think logically and handle abstract concepts.

Ask your child open ended questions that would make him reflect on the subject of money; lead him to form his opinion about money.

Let money alone not determine his choice of profession; professions that contribute so much to society such as teaching should be held in high regard, instead of professions that command high income. We are the ones that give value to money and not the other way round.

You can express love through monetary gifts to a person in need, however, your child should be taught that there are non-monetary ways of showing love such as spending time with a loved one who is sick in the hospital.

Conflicts do arise in connection with use of money; for instance monetary gifts for public officers are deemed inappropriate because it can compromises them in the discharge of their duties.

It therefore means that there are occasions when money can be given as well occasions when giving money is inappropriate.

How to Teach Your Child Money Management Skills

Children need to be taught skills on handling money in an age-appropriate manner. Guide and advise your child on issues about money instead of dictating what to do to him; in this way he learns by doing. Encourage and praise him when he does the right thing, empathize with him when he makes mistakes since he is on a learning curve. Create boundaries on what he can and cannot do as far as money is concerned.

Help him develop good spending habit. Give your child allowance and supervise its use. Such allowance given to a child is meant to teach him about responsible money management. This benefit stops once he starts earning.

Help him develop a saving habit. Teach him to save for what he wants; help him open a bank account to introduce him to a saving culture.

Get him involved in family budget discussions. Let him get a hands-on exposure to the dynamics of financing a family. Share your challenges with your child so that he would know that life is not a bed of roses.

Teach him how to give away money wisely. Get him to give money to charity and other worthy causes to sensitize him to the needs of the underprivileged.

Teach him to be generous. Tell him that the law of sowing and reaping is real. Tell him that those who always give never lack. The Dead Sea is a dead sea because it takes everything but gives nothing out.

Allow him pay bills on your behalf. This would expose him to economics of daily living. Let him know that some of the most constant things in life are bills and taxes; therefore money must be well managed at all times to enable you fulfill these obligations.

Teach him to earn his own money. He will get to know that a lot goes into making money while spending money is a lot easier.

Tell him about your investments. This will enable him know that it is always good to save for the rainy day. Investments are the outcome of disciplined spending as well as financial intelligence.

When not to give money. Do not use money as an inducement for household chores. That is a child's input to the household. Do not use money as an inducement for better academic performance at school. Better grades should bring inner satisfaction and be seen as a reward of hard work. Money as an inducement for better grades gives the erroneous impression that money can buy all things including love etc. **Teach him to identify requests for unworthy causes which should not be granted.** Requests that fund establishment of abortion clinics should be turned down.

Let your moral values guide you in your patronage of company products. Tell him why you don't buy products of companies that use child labour because it is against what you stand for.

Express your desire to have things you cannot afford for now. Your children should know that you say "no" to yourself on some things you cannot presently afford. You are teaching them how to delay gratification.

Tell them about contentment and ambition. Contentment is being satisfied with what you have for the moment and trying to live within your means. Ambition on the other hand is a compelling desire to make money at all costs and this may make a person compromise on his moral values.

IN A NUTSHELL

1. Money matters matter greatly in daily living; you need to help your child develop skills in handling money.

2. Start from infancy and give your child the right orientation about money. Help him shape his attitude about money.

LIFE APPLICATION

1. What pleasant and unpleasant experiences have you had with money that your child can learn from?

2. In what ways do you model "living within" your means to your child?

3. Can you use real life situations to explain the differences between needs and wants to your child?

FURTHER READING

Danes, S.M. 1991 "Money, Kids, and Allowances." *Young Families Newsletter.*100 Minnesota Extension Service: St Paul

Felder, L.1990. "Money wise kids: Teach kids early to save, earn and spend sensibly." *Parents,* 65(5), 233-240

Waddell, F.E. 1985. *Money and your children.* Genesis Press: Baton Rouge

Walker R. and I. Hathaway, 1991. *Helping your child learn to manage money.* NCR392. Michigan Extension Service and North Central Region Publication, USDA.

CHAPTER TWENTY-TWO
Time Management Skills

FOCUSING QUESTIONS

1. *Why is time important?*

2. *What are the time wasting activities of children?*

3. *What are some time management skills you can teach your child?*

WHY TIME IS ALWAYS OF YHE ESSENCE

Time is always of the essence for the following reasons:

Time is a limited resource What you have to do in this limited time could be gargantuan; yet you have all the time you need to do what you have to do. Effective time management enables you to accomplish all there is to do in the available time.

Time lost cannot be retrieved The past is gone; the future may not come so you must maximize the time you have at hand. There is often a wide disparity between the way you think you spend your time and the way you actually spend your time. Evaluating the time taken to do necessary tasks would enable you see things in the right perspective.

"Dost thou love life? Then do not squander time, for that is the stuff life is made of."

Benjamin Franklin

BASIC PRINCIPLES OF TIME MANAGEMENT

Before you can effectively manage your time, you must consider the following:

How much time do you have?

1. The list of things you have to do must be classified into those that are urgent and those that can wait

2. How to accomplish all you want to do in the available time.

ADVANTAGES OF TIME MANAGEMENT

1.You are at peace with your self when you are in control of your time; you are able to manage your life better because you do what you want to do with minimal stress and without unnecessary dissipation of energy. 2 You accomplish much because your time is shared between household chores, school and play activities. 3. You are able to establish balance between school work, personal affairs and household commitments 4 You are well positioned to respond to any challenges or new opportunities that might arise because you make time available from your schedule.

PRACTICAL WAYS BY WHICH YOU CAN HELP YOUR CHILD MANAGE HIS TIME

1. **Use a to-do list to write down what you plan to do in a day.** This enables you to keep all you need to do each day or each week in your full view. The list might consist of

    a   What you want to do at home

    b   What you want to do at school

    c   Laundry and sundry activities

    d   Leisure activities

2. **Prioritize your list** Decide on what to give more time to or spend less time on. Let basic things like eating, sleeping have their slot, followed by school assignments and household chores; attend to issues that have deadlines. You may determine how important something is by imagining the consequences of not doing such things.

3. **Plan your week [Daily or weekly planner].** You increase your productivity when you plan your week's activities ahead because you are able to balance long term commitments against urgent tasks.   1.**Use a time budget** This requires allotting time to all your activities of the day for a 24 hour time frame. Below is an example

Time Allotted

Sleep   7 Hours
School / lessons 9 Hours
Meals 1 Hour
Shower / preparation for school ½ hour
Household chores 1 Hour
Homework 2 Hours

Studying 2 Hours
Television 1 Hour
Recreation ½ Hour
TOTAL 24 HOURS

5. **Learn to say No and not feel guilty.** The truth is there are more activities competing for your time than the amount of time you have. When you learn to say no without feeling guilty, you have delivered yourself from a common bondage that many persons get into. Say no to low priority requests.

6. **Keep a pocket notebook.** When a helpful thought comes to your mind write it down before you forget it.

Think before you act or commit your time. Learn to look at your list of things to do before accepting new commitments.

1. **Cut down on time spent on TV/ Internet / magazine.** This will allow you more time to do the needful.

2. **Use a time log to assess how effective you are at managing time.** This will enable you make the needed adjustments to achieve your goal.

3. **Develop blocks of study time.** For how long can you read before you become restless or go for break?

4. **Do Multiple Tasks** If you have to do outdoor tasks, take all the outdoor tasks in one swoop. For instance, you can clean the car, empty the garbage and clean the dog kernel.

5. **Make your household chores fun.** See if you can improve on your speed of doing the same thing to the same standard. You may dance and sing

while doing vacuum or cleaning the car.

6. **Have a weekly review of your activities.** See how much progress you are making.

7. **Identify your time-wasting habits.** Work on such habits or replace them with good habits. If you take too long to shower, cut down on the time you take.

8. **Tap into your energy cycles.** Identify the time of the day you are most productive and use that time to do your complex and challenging tasks.

9. **Maintain a clean desk.** Remove unnecessary items from your desk to spare you any distractions.

10. **Make out time for recreation** This enables you to feel refreshed and re-fired for any task you want to do.

11. **Quit Day-Dreaming.** Use your time well on tangible issues instead of fantasizing.

12. **Create a check list for repeat task.** This makes it easy for you to build into your routine.

13. **Get enough sleep.** This will make you very alert mentally, so you can cover a lot of grounds in a short time.

14. **Setting goals.** This can be divided into what you want to do in a matter of hours or couple of days as well as what you want to do in a matter of months.

15. **Break up big assignments into smaller bits.** This is good for long term assignments or projects.

"Waste your money and you're only out of money, but waste your time and you're lost a part of your life."

Michael Leboeuf

TIME WASTERS IN CHILDREN

The following are some common time wasters:

A. **Procrastination** Learn to do what you have to do immediately.

B **Whining and complaining** This takes your time while the task is left undone.

C **TV, the phone and the internet**. Allot time to these ones. Do not do your homework while listening to music.

D **Too many leisure activities** Learn to play only after you have done what needs to be done.

HOW TO KNOW WHEN YOUR TIME IS OVERLOADED

If you have too many activities cramped into your day, your time is being over loaded; you need to shed some of your activities. This is how you know you are being over loaded:

1. You lose interest in your activities because of the stress.

2. Your eyes are constantly on the clock.

3. You are always rushing from one activity to the other.

4. You are finding it hard to meet your target.

5. You feel caged in almost to the point of suffocation.

In a Nutshell

1. Time is a very valuable but limited resource that moves slowly but passes quickly. When you maximize your use of time, you have a lot of things to show for it.

2. There are hosts of ways by which children and teens can develop time management skills once the desire to do so is there.

Life Application

1. What activities can you identify that drain your child's time mostly? How do you plan to help him overcome this challenge?

2. In what areas of your life can you model good time management skills to your child?

Further Reading

1. Stephen Covey (1990) *The Seven habits of Highly Successful People* [Fireside]

2. Axelrod, A; Holtje (19970): *201 Ways to Manage Your Time Better* [MacGraw-Hill]

3. Vienne ,V; Lennard, E (1998): *The Art of Doing Nothing: Simple Ways to Make Time for Yourself* [Clarkson Potter]

4. Mind Tools E-book available at http://www.mindtools.com

5. Master Your Time e-Book available at http://www.MasterYourTimeNow.com

6 Achieve Planner Software available at http://www.effexis.com/achieve/planner.htm

CHAPTER TWENTY-THREE

Gender Issues: True Masculinity and True Feminity

FOCUSING QUESTIONS

1. *What is true masculinity?*

2. *What are the challenges youths face that make them require real men and women as mentors?*

3. *What are the attributes of real men?*

4. *What are the attributes of real women?*

TRUE MASCULINITY

There are so many discordant voices when it comes to defining what true masculinity is. For some it is heavy beard, good looks, hand and neck chains, and well developed physique which are just phenotypic expression of the masculine gender. A father is called to model what true masculinity is to his sons. Fathers should provide manhood training for their sons while mothers should model true feminity for their daughters at an age they are most impressionable. The bible in Mal 4:5-6 describes what God would do in respect of father-child relationship in these words "He will restore the hearts of the fathers to their children and the hearts of the children to their fathers".

True masculinity is defined by emotional competence which is the ability to manage your emotion in a healthy and productive manner, self-regulated behaviour as well as a having a good personal value system.

Fathers are in a position to pass on to sons, the wisdom that comes with age and experience in a comfortable home environment. Your sons, because of the time they have been with you at home are likely to take after you especially if you had a good relationship with them. According to Robert Lewis, "Men assume social responsibility most naturally and effectively when it is clear to them that the primary responsibility for the well being of others rests on them and that others are relying on them. Secondly when they have been trained from an early age by the men in their lives to recognize and assume that responsibility faithfully".

Boys who were not mentored by their fathers either pick up a feminized version of masculinity from their mothers or a perverted image of masculinity from their peers. It is trite to say that while mothers raise boys, it takes fathers to raise men.

Real men are those who display all the attributes of mature and responsible manhood.

"There is no royal road to anything, one thing at a time, all things in succession. That which grows fast withers as rapidly. That which grows slowly endures."

Josiah Gilbert Holland

REASONS WHY TEENAGERS REQUIRE REAL MEN AND WOMEN AS MENTORS

The following are the reasons why teenagers require real men and women as mentors:

Impulsiveness Young persons very often leap before they look because to a lot of them all that glitters is gold. Only those who can think critically and are able to sift the chaff from the wheat exercise due restraint in taking important decisions.

A strong desire for independence This makes them want to behave as adult by taking decisions that could affect them adversely.

Peer pressure Youths would want to act like their peers so that they would be accepted in the fold.

They want to be popular and noticed This has a way of massaging their ego, especially when the self-validation that ought to have come from their parents is missing.

Tendency towards rebellion This tendency expresses itself when they want to go against what they have been taught to be acceptable.

Popular culture Teens are often tempted to act in consonance with what everybody is doing even if that thing is wrong.

Moral decadence A decadent world makes it necessary for young persons to have people they can talk with and whose words they will follow.

CHARACTERISTICS OF REAL MEN

The following are some of the attributes of real men:

A real man loves Jesus. To him, Jesus epitomizes true masculinity in His love for mankind which made him shed his blood for humanity. He models his life after that of Jesus.

A real man accepts responsibility for his actions. It is reasonably true that everyman is the architect of his own fortune or misfortune. A responsible person faces the consequences of his actions. He does not take refuge in denial. Tell your son that the entirety of an adult's life is made of personal choices, decisions and their consequences. Somehow a man will reap what he sows- that is how fair life is. The way you lay your bed is how you will lie on it. Remember Shakespeare's words "Men at sometime are masters of their own fate".

A real man is accountable for his actions. Stewardship is always demanded of persons in position of authority to whom much has been given. You are expected to use all resources committed to your care judiciously and render an account when asked to do so. Trust and responsibility define accountability. Tell your son that financial profligacy is a prescription for a life of penury. A man who cannot or does not have a saving culture but spends all he earns will be a slave to money lending institutions.

A real man is dedicated to truth. It is noble to seek the truth at all times and to live by it. Truth has a liberating power on those who abide by it. You need a life of total honesty and constant self- examination to stay in the truth. Truth is constant and always stands the test of time.

Tell your son that there is nothing hidden that would not be revealed at some point in time. He should never take part in a shady deal because the long arm of the law sooner or later catches up with criminals. Honesty remains the best policy in life.

A real man can stand alone when an occasion calls for it. There comes a time when you need to stand alone on issues that border on values that are dear to you. That everybody is doing something does not make it right; majority does not carry the day on moral issues. Be willing to take your stand on issues that border on morality because of your strong convictions. You need a good measure of self- confidence and self- esteem to stand alone.

Tell your son that a person who cannot stand alone on a major issue would fall for anything.

A real man exercises self-control over his behaviour and emotions. He maintains balance in all he does and in whatever position he takes on an issue. He can laugh freely and cry when overwhelmed by emotions without feeling less of a man. He shares his feelings with his wife and children without thinking that he will lose their respect. Under crisis situations, he maintains his cool while fashioning out an appropriate response. He has built his own personal reinforcement system such that problems are seen as challenges to be surrounded. He does not require stimulants such as tobacco, alcohol or hard drugs to live a normal life.

A real man is at peace with his gender. He is happy being a man and does not fantasize with being a woman. Weaving of hair, wearing of ear rings or piercing his nose to look like a woman is not for him.

A real man strives to achieve excellence in whatever is committed to him. He has a good work ethic and enjoys his work.

A real man exhibits strength of character. He is a change agent who believes he is a tool to make the world a better place. He is not blown around by every wind of doctrine or philosophy. Words cannot break the bones of a real man.

A real man considers marriage as sacred and gives it priority.

He marries for life; loves and honours his wife above all else and treats her like a queen. He provides for his wife's physical, spiritual, emotional and sexual needs. He literally lays his life down for his family when it comes to providing for them and protecting them from harm. He manages his sexuality well and does not sow wild oats.

A real man honours and respects all women. He does not strike women rather he protects them from physical harm because he is the stronger sex. He protects ladies as the weaker vessel. He does not exploit them or play on their emotions.

A real man is focused. He does not waste valuable time pursuing different goals without achieving anything. He differentiates the important from the mundane and gives it all it takes to achieve predetermined goals.

A real man's word is his bond. He says what he means and means what he says without being caught in a web of verbosity. He can be taken for his word. He does not promise what he cannot deliver.

A real man is role model in every sense for the younger generation. He epitomizes true masculinity in his values and lifestyle. He has good leadership and communication skills.

A real man has a genuine source of income. Makes his own living from a salaried job or business. He is neither a loafer nor a drifter; he is in touch with reality.

A real man is law abiding. He follows the rule of law in his affairs. He does not lie, steal or cheat in his affairs. He pays his taxes and bills as and when due.

"One of life's greatest mysteries is how the boy who wasn't good enough to marry your daughter can be the father of the smartest grandchild in the world."

Jewish Proverb

CHARACTERISTICS OF A REAL WOMAN

A real woman loves Jesus. She believes in God, loves His word, is prayerful and lives a godly life.

A real woman has a good personal value system. She is decent, loving, truthful, gentle and compassionate.

A real woman celebrates her feminity. She loves womanhood, likes being a woman, behaves like a lady, cherishes her feminity and sees herself as special.

A real woman is an asset to her husband [Proverbs 31:10-31] She respects her husband and treats him like her king. She supports her husband in all he does, is a hard worker and is trustworthy. She would not eat the bread of idleness.

A real woman builds her home. She would not sacrifice her home for her job. She loves and cares for her children and makes the home environment attractive for all the family.

A real woman cherishes good character more than beauty. She recognizes goodness, admires godly women, delights in truth and beauty, respects herself and other people; she is generous with compliments and easily pleased. She is not quarrelsome neither does she engage in gossips.

A real woman is decent. She understands chastity, values her sexuality, controls her passions and desires because she knows her body is the temple of the Holy Spirit.

A real woman pays attention to her physical looks. She is well groomed in appearance, keeps herself in shape, modest in dressing and does not play on the emotions of men.

A real woman is a paragon of virtues. She loves goodness and exhibits it in all her dealings.

IN A NUTSHELL

1. Real men do not merely have the physical characteristics of the male gender but are self-regulated in their behaviour while exhibiting godly character in their lives.

2. Teenagers need significant persons who are either their parents, uncles or teachers who will model what true masculinity or feminity is.

3. True feminity transcends physical beauty; it is defined by strong moral values, industry and family values.

146

LIFE APPLICATION

1. Have you had an occasion to talk with your son on one on one basis about true masculinity? You need to do so before his peers lure him to experimentation with sex or drugs. You might feel awkward doing this especially if you do not talk to him about moral issues; however let your sense of responsibility override this feeling.

2. You must create time also to talk with your daughter about true feminity and why it is important for her to develop those virtues and values that will make her stand out among her peers.

FURTHER READING

Edwin Louis Cole, *Maximized Manhood*

The Bible, Proverbs 31:10-31[New King James Version]

CHAPTER TWENTY-FOUR
Preventing Teenage Parenthood

FOCUSING QUESTIONS

1. *Why teenage parenthood should be prevented?*

2. *What are the causes of teenage parenthood?*

3. *What measures can a father take to prevent teenage parenthood?*

THE PROBLEM OF TEENAGE PARENTHOOD

1. Teenage parenthood is one of the social maladies of this age. Children from all social classes have at one time or the other been caught in this web. The United States has the highest rate of teen pregnancy in the industrialized world with 34% of girls getting pregnant at least once before the age of 20. After increasing 23% between 1972 and 1990 [including 10% between 1987 and 1990, the teen pregnancy rate for girls aged 15-19 decreased 28% between 1990 and 2000 to a record low [Henshaw S (2003) US pregnancy statistics with comparative statistics for women aged 20-24 New York The Alan Gattmacher].

2. Teenage parenthood brings untold hardship to the newborn child, causes a great setback to the teenage mother, leaves a scar on the teenage father, brings embarrassment on the parents on both sides and is a drain on the resources of society.

3. In view of the above consequences of teenage parenthood, every father has a responsibility of preparing his sons and daughters to delay sexual activity till marriage. Measures that have been found effective in achieving this goal are those put in place in the preteen and early teen years before the child gets exposed to this challenge.

A father can do this through communication, helping his child develop a good personal value system, helping his child with acquisition of life skills and choice of friends.

Teenage Fathers

Several studies have found them to be:

A Totally absent from the lives of their children either due to conflicts with the mother of their child or because of inability to provide for their child.

B Responsible for sole motherhood and all the problems associated with it. Society blames them for causing the problem and fleeing-"In the light of the fact that most sexual activity is male initiated, and most sexual behaviour is male influenced, it becomes clear that there will be no resolution of the problem of teenage pregnancy without directing greater attention to the male" [E. Pitt(1986)].

C 30% of teenage fathers have low self image [Jones M 2000]. They are prone to parental failure because they would be grappling with developmental tasks of adolescence and responsibilities of fatherhood at the same time.

D Early fatherhood has been found to be determined by the family of origin and individual characteristics of the teenager.

Teenage Motherhood results in less formal educational attainment because of the disruption of schooling that results from pregnancy and child rearing.

Higher probability of divorce among parents who chose to marry because the marriage was not planned; rather it was undertaken to hide their shame.

Poverty in later life because of poor educational attainment which limits opportunities for well paying jobs later in life.

CAUSES OF TEENAGE PARENTHOOD

Some of the causes of teenage parenthood are:

Poor parent-child relationship that did not allow the child to disclose pressures he/she is going through. Adolescence is a high tension period that is characterized by severe mood swings, feelings of loneliness and struggles with relationships. Teenagers become more curious about their body changes and would want independence from parents as well as self-gratification from sexual experimentation. Some girls who have poor relationship with their parents may see getting pregnant as an assertion of their independence. Some girls see pregnancy as a form of rebellion against parents who were too strict and did not give them enough freedom to do what they liked. Such girls may choose to raise

their children in a way that gives the child plenty of freedom, reflecting the lifestyle they had wished they had while growing up. Research has found the following; "The more teenagers are satisfied with the mother-child relationship, the less likely they are to be sexually experienced [Advocates for Youth, 1997]. Conversely, poor communication with parents about sex and safe sex practices, and parental substance abuse are also linked with risky sexual behaviours" (Fraser,1997). Poor parent-child relationships are associated with depression in adolescents. For young men, this may lead to more frequent use of alcohol, which is strongly linked to early sexual activity.

1 **Lack of moral instructions in the pre-teen and teenage years.** Poor parental supervision of their children which can arise from both parents working for most of the day paves the way for the development of negative behaviour in children. Adolescents have much time to explore premarital sexual activities that can eventually lead to pregnancy. You hear statements like "My mother was never home. And when she finally decided to start caring, it was already too late"[Gholston 1997]

2 **Lack of sexuality instructions.** This result in teens getting inaccurate information from their peers that encourage them to experiment with sex. A study by Kaiser Foundation found "Teenagers are most likely to seek sexual information from their friends [61%]. Although they are least likely to seek information from their parents[32%], a significant number of teenagers[43%] express a strong

desire to have more information on how to talk to their parents about sex and relationships"[Kaiser Family Foundation, 2000].

3 **Lack of good role models** Having good role models whom young girls can relate to prevents them from searching for answers to life's puzzles on their own. In this way, they get good counsel that tells them not to experiment with sex.

4 **Being raised in single parent families.** Children from this background lack a strong personal value system that can shield them from sexual exploitation

5 **Sexual exploitation of minors by older persons.** Parents should have a high index of suspicion of males around the home who can exploit their daughters. Studies have shown that many cases of sexual exploitation are from persons known to the victim.

6 **Peer pressure from bad company.** Teenagers should be taught to avoid bad company especially the company of persons who indulge in or believe in premarital sex. Youths who resist engaging in sexual activity tend to have friends who are abstinent as well; they also tend to have strong personal beliefs in abstinence and the perception of negative parent reactions. Youths who are sexually active tend to believe that most of their friends are sexually active as well, that rewards outweigh the costs of sexual involvement, that sex overall is rewarding, and that it is alright for unmarried adolescents over age 16 to engage in intercourse(Advocates for Youth, 1997)

7 **Sexual assaults and date-raping.** Teenage girls should be told of the very high incidence of date rape so that they can put necessary measures in place to avoid being taken advantage of.

8 **Watching sexually explicit movies and pornography.** Sexual innuendoes in advertisements play on the emotions of adolescents and this could heighten interest in sexual exploration. In the U.S, more than half [56 percent] of all television shows contain sexual content-averaging more than three scenes with sex per hour. For shows with sexual content, just 9 percent include any mention of the possible risks of sexual activity, or any reference to contraception, protection, or safer sex [Kaiser Family foundation, 1999]. Among young people 10 to 17 years of age who regularly use the internet, one quarter had been exposed to unwanted pornography in the past year, and one-fifth had been exposed to unwanted sexual solicitations or approaches [U.S. Public Health Service, 2001].

9 **Some teenage mothers see their babies as their only source of love and attention and so go for it.** Teenage girls should be told that the best interests of the new born baby should be considered before choosing to be pregnant. Babies need the security of a family and working parent(s) to provide adequately for them.

"We have to learn to be our own best friends because we fall too

easily into the trap of being our own worst enemies."

Roderick Thorpe

STRATEGIES FOR PREVENTING TEENAGE PARENTHOOD

A. Delaying first sexual experience

Relating to first sexual experience various researchers have found the following:

1 Teenagers that have sex in their early teens and later have more sexual partners are less likely to use contraceptive and more likely to get pregnant. For example, 1 in 7 sexually experienced young teen become pregnant by age 15.

2 Teens that first had sex at an early age are more likely to have older partners.

3 Many girls who had sex at a young age report that their first sexual experience was coercive.

4 Boys in general and youth of racial and ethnic minority groups in the US tend to have first sex at younger ages than girls and non-Hispanic white teens.

5 Youths whose mothers were teen mothers and those with sexually experienced or pregnant siblings are also more likely to have sex early.

6 The above findings would help in designing intervention measures that would help teens at risk for teenage parenthood.

Preventive measures include:

A. **Educated two parent families** Research has found that having a 2 parent family and or parents with high levels of education and income are associated with teens delaying their first sexual encounter. Therefore, work at sustaining a good relationship with your wife since divorce worsens the lot of children in this regard.

B. **High quality parent-teen relationships help delay sexual initiation.** Teens who feel they have a high quality relationship with their parents and whose parents communicate strong disapproval of sexual activity are more likely to delay sex. Also teens whose parents closely monitor their behaviour through supervision and rules about dating and social activities also report delay in first sexual encounter. Excessive parental control on the other hand can be associated with problem behaviours in teenagers. A U.S Public Health report stated that "For young women, estrangement at home often leads them to seek and establish intimate relationships outside the family, seeking the warmth and support they lack at home. Among girls experiencing sexual abuse in the family are linked, an increased risk of teenage pregnancy" [U.S. Public Health service, 2001]

C. **Make your child develop the right attitude to sex**. Sex is not for recreation nor can it be experimented with; it should be reserved for marriage. When adolescents are convinced that sex is for married persons and move with peers who share the same belief, they are able to delay their first sexual encounter till marriage.

D. **Put your child in a good quality school** Schools have unique opportunities to provide information as well as structured activities that discourage involvement in premarital sex. Greater involvement in school is related to decrease in sexual risk taking and later initiation of sex, pregnancy, and childbearing (US Public Health Service, 2001).

E. **Virginity pledge** Taking a virginity pledge has been found to delay having a first sexual encounter.

F. **Shunning romantic relationships for a season** Postponing having a steady romantic relationship till a person is ready for marriage helps in delaying first sexual encounter. Teens who have dated or who say they have been in a romantic relationship are more likely to have early sex. Dating an older partner is also linked to having first sex at a younger age.

G. **Pursuing academic excellence** Passion for excellence in academic work at school and moving with peers that share similar goals also leads to delay in first sexual encounter. Young women who were the least successful in high school are the most likely to become pregnant [National Association of Social Workers(NASW),2000]

11. **Avoiding risky behaviours** Teens who do not indulge in risky behaviours such as drinking, taking drugs of addiction, smoking, indulging in pornography and who also do not keep the company of peers who do such things are able to delay their first sexual encounter. Substance use and abuse are also factors in sexual decision making. One quarter of sexually active high school youths reported using alcohol or drugs during their most recent sexual encounter(Kaiser Family Foundation,2000)

I. **Protect your children** Protecting children from sexual abuse delays first sexual encounter.

J. **Sporting activities** Involvement in competitive sports also leads to delay in

first sexual encounter because it provides avenues for channeling youthful energies.

K. **Gainful Employment for Youths** Unemployment, difficulties in accessing further education and overall social disintegration are associated with higher sexual risk taking.[Fraser,1997]

B. Involvement in church and religious activities

This has a way of building the spiritual and moral life of the teenager to the extent that sexual experimentation may not appeal to the teen. Group activities have a way of bringing together teens of similar persuasion and this helps in reinforcing their conviction of delaying sex till marriage. The bible forbids premarital sex; a teen that knows the bible and follows its precepts early in life will have the inner strength to say no to sexual experimentation.

C. Communication

From the preteen years, start talking to your child about the importance of developing moral values and how to stay chaste.

Teach your child that abstinence is the best preventive measure for teenage parenthood as well as sexually transmitted diseases.

Teach your child how to draw the line in a relationship with the opposite sex and respect the line. Living a respectful and respectable life would shield a child from teenage parenthood.

Teaching your child to be honest in talking with you will make you know what is going on in his/her life.

Children must be taught what good choices are and how to make them. The ability to stand alone if need be on moral issues must be well communicated to your children.

It does not matter what others do or say; what matters is what you chose to do or say.

D. Sexuality Education

Giving your children human sexuality education arms them with accurate knowledge of how their body functions and prevents them from falling prey to wrong information peddled by their peers to lure them in to early sexual encounter. Nearly 80 percent of teenagers indicate that what their parents have told them and what their parents might think influence their decisions about sex and their relationships [Kaiser Family Foundation,2000].

E. Youth Involvement in development programs

Programs that teach life skills, career explorations and education enhancement divert teenage minds from sexual activities to purposeful, life transforming activities that help to develop them.

Programs that encourage teens to practice important negotiation and sex refusal skills through role-playing have been found to be very effective in reducing risky sexual behaviour.

Programs that teach teenagers how to render public service or render volunteer works help them in channeling their energy in to creative activities that help society

F. Helping your child choose good friends

Making friends is part of the developmental tasks of adolescence. Friends are important, even needed by everyone; however a lot of persons can trace their woes in life to having chosen bad friends.

Choosing friends can be difficult because a lot of persons are not who they pretend to be. The bible in 1Corinthian 15:33 says "Bad company corrupts good morals". Someone has defined a friend as someone who comes in when the whole world has gone out.

Friends have a lot of influence on each other, a common saying sums it all; "Show me your friend and I will tell you who you are". Friends have a way of mirroring each other.

How a father can help his child choose good friends

Parents have been found to affect their children indirectly by shaping their choice of friends. They can do this in practical ways by:

Having a warm relationship with your child that is defined by doing things together, good communication and expression of affection for each other.

Choosing to live in a decent neighbourhood with high quality schools so that your child can have better opportunities to have good friends.

1 Asking your child to bring his/her friends home so you can monitor and supervise his/her choice of friends. Research has found that parental familiarity with children's friends made the friends have more pro-social activities.

2 Get to know the parents of your child's friends also; it makes the children feel you have high expectations of their relationship

3 It has been found that teens with more autonomy have more delinquent

friends, so be on the alert. Do not give your child more freedom than he requires for his age. 4 Use teachable moments to talk to your child about the nitty gritty of friendship such as:

5 Choosing friends who share similar personal values with you. This is because friends can influence you for good or for evil

6 here is give and take in friendship, so make sure you make wise choices. Improve on your social skills so that you can retain your friends.

7 Choose friends who do not have self destructive habits like violence, smoking, drinking, examination malpractice, or who indulge in pornography.

8 Some of your friends may have qualities you admire that you do not have.

9 Honesty is important in friendship. You can have many friends; good friends make you feel good about yourself.

10 Spending time together with your friend helps your relationship to grow.

11 Friends may hurt you at times or you may have disagreements so you must learn to forgive or overlook the shortcomings of your friend.

12 You can be friends with the opposite gender, it can be a platonic relationship and not necessarily romantic.

"Associate yourself with men of good quality if you esteem your reputation; for it is better to be alone than in bad company".
George Washington

G Monitor your child's TV viewing

A Rand survey published in the September 2004 issue of Pediatrics found that teens that are more exposed to TV sexual content are twice more likely to have sex than those with less exposure. TV programs with abundant sexual content should be shunned because they create illusion that sex is more central to daily life than it is truly and this may promote teenage sex experimentation.

IN A NUTSHELL

1. Teenage parenthood affects children from all social class; every teenager is vulnerable and must be protected.

2. Teenage parenthood affects the lives of teens and their babies adversely.

3. There are many causes of teenage parenthood and prominent among them is poor parent-child relationship.

4. There are various strategies that can be used to prevent this problem.

LIFE APPLICATION

1 Have you given your teenager sexuality education that explains how his/her body works and explained the dangers of teenage parenthood?

2 How open is your relationship with your child? Have you conveyed to him/her your wish that sexual activity should be delayed till marriage?

3 Do you know your child's closest friends? You can ask your child to bring his/her friend home so you can interact with him/her.

FURTHER READING

James Lindsay: *Parents, Pregnant Teens and the Adoption Option*. Harold J. Sala; *Raising Godly Kid* Alan Guttmacher Institute (AGI), 1999. *Fact Sheet on Teen Sex and Pregnancy*

Advocates for Youth.(1997). *Fact sheet on Adolescent Sexual Behaviour:II. Sociopsychological Factors*

Fraser M,.(1997) *Risk and resilience in Childhood: An Ecological perspective*. Washington,DC: NASW Press

Kaiser Family Foundation, *Decision-Making about Sex: SexSmarts,* 2000b

National Association of Social Workers. (2000). *Adolescent Pregnancy and Parenting: Social work speaks: National Association of Social Workers Policy Statements 2000-2003(pp.15)* Washington, DC:NASW Press

U.S. Public Health Service, *The Surgeon General's Call to Action to Promote Sexual Health and Responsible Behaviour*. Washington, DC:2001

CHAPTER TWENTY-FIVE
Teen Health and Leisure Activities

FOCUSING QUESTIONS

1. *Why is teen health important?*
2. *What are the health issues peculiar to teenagers?*

THE IMPORTANCE OF TEEN HEALTH

Health according to the World Health Organization is not "the absence of disease but a state of physical, social and mental well being." It is good for teens to know the health challenges that might confront them so that early in life, they would put in place measures that would enable them enjoy good health.

TEEN NUTRITION

Nutrition this entails taking the right quantity and quality of food. Over nutrition has as much deleterious effect on health as under nutrition. Ailments such as anorexia nervosa and bulimia are disorders of nutrition that are more common among young females than young males.

Proper nutrition helps in building a teenager's immune system. A personal habit of watching what to eat lays a good foundation for sustainable health in later years of life.

Obesity with its myriad of comorbid conditions is a common problem of this generation. Junk foods and lack of exercise fuel the rising incidence of this condition.

A healthy diet must have the following:

Enough calories from carbohydrate to provide energy for growth and other activities. Sources of calories must include complex carbohydrates, grains, legumes, cereals, potatoes, yams and whole wheat products.

Enough proteins to build new tissues. Adolescence is a period of rapid growth that requires a lot of protein intake. Sources of protein are meat, beans, fish, eggs, Soya beans etc, etc

Take a lot of vitamins, minerals and micro-nutrients to keep your body cells functioning optimally.

Take enough fibres to ensure proper bowel movement and prevent constipation.

Eat plenty of fruits and vegetables- the goal should be to take at least 5 portions a day.

Drink up to 1 pint of low fat milk daily.

Obesity It is excess body fat that affects the health of the person resulting in reduced life expectancy. Body Mass Index [BMI] which is used in measuring the degree of obesity compares a person's weight and height. The normal BMI is less than $25kg/M^2$, a rate of 25 to 30 is overweight while above 30 is obesity.

Strategies for avoiding obesity

A Take responsibility for what you choose to eat.

B Cut down on intake of foods and drinks that are high in sugars e.g. sweets, soda, soft drinks, cakes and biscuits.

C Reduce fried foods intake such as egg, bacon, meat, and fish.

D Do not eat any meals especially heavy meals after 7 pm.

E Exercise regularly.

F Limit time spent on watching TV, surfing the net, playing computer and video games.

G Separate TV watching time from meal times. You easily over eat while watching the TV or surfing the net.

H Exercise discipline in eating; eat only when you are hungry; do not eat to overcome depression.

I Snack on low sugar fruits instead of cookies.

EXERCISE

This does a world of good to teenagers; it is a key for looking good and feeling great for the rest of life. It is the single best route to a long and active life.

What are the benefits of exercise?

1 It keeps you fit and conveys a sense of wellness to you. It keeps your body trim, your muscles toned and your posture straight. It gives you a confident gait.

2 Regular exercise will give you physical, emotional and mental power to cope with daily living. Your staying-power in any giving situation is amplified by exercise.

3 Exercise has positive impart on your health. It helps prevent while it is part of the treatment for diseases such as stroke, heart diseases, diabetes mellitus, arthritis, cancer and osteoporosis. If you have an underlying health condition, it may be necessary to see your doctor for advice on what type of exercise is right for you.

4 It helps you control your weight by burning off calories. Exercise has been found to be as effective as dieting in weight control.

5 Exercise produces mental alertness which enables you to look forward to an exciting day.

6 A study carried out by Melissa Nelson, RD of University of Minnesota and Penny Gordon-Larsen PhD of University of North Carolina at Chapel Hill found that physically active teenagers are less likely to engage in risky behaviour [like smoking, drinking and sex] and are more likely to have positive traits[such as better self-esteem, higher grades and more sleep].

7 Rick Bell, professor of Physical Education says "The academic benefits of being physically fit have been researched quite extensively and studies show that when time is allocated on a daily basis to exercise, there is no negative impact on the academic achievement of children. Typically, children who are active have more energy and can concentrate more, so it makes better use of the time used for academic achievement in our schools."

A list of exercises to choose from:

1 Walking -This is safe and beneficial for virtually all age groups. Walk instead of driving or park at a distance and walk the rest of the way; take the stairs instead of using the elevator all the time.

2 Jogging or running

3 Swimming and water exercise- This is meant for those who can swim and is very beneficial for those with arthritis.

4 Cycling

5 Dancing

6 Exercise classes with instructors on hand

7 Weight training- This is good for strengthening and conditioning of muscles

8 Exercise videos- You can purchase your own or tune in to cable fitness channel.

"There is no friendship, no love like that of the parent for the child."

Henry Ward Beecher

KEEPING FIT MENTALLY THROUGH PROPER HANDLING OF STRESS

Stress is one of the greatest threats to stable mental health in teenagers. Stress can be defined as your mind and body response to any new, threatening or challenging situation. Stress provokes a reaction from your body that enables you overcome a threatening situation, a physical challenge, solve problems, reach set goals or flee from danger. When stress continues for a long period of time, it can have some adverse effects on your health such as headache, loss of appetite, sleeplessness, depression and other physical problems.

Causes of stress in preteens and teenagers include the following:

School demands and home work

Poor academic performance

High parental expectations

Too many activities like lessons, co-curricular activities

Conflict with parents

Conflict between parents

Conflict with friends

Financial problems at home Breaking up with friends

Divorce between parents

Change of schools

Pubertal changes

Peer pressure to join a bad gang Bullying at school

Weight concern and body image

Stress lowering measures include the following:

Eat right; take a lot of fruits and vegetables while avoiding excessive sugar and fat.

Exercise regularly

Get plenty of sleep

Take time to relax.

Turn in your assignments when due Maintaining good academic performance through consistent reading and use of good study techniques.

Having good recreation activities to unwind after a day's work.

Keeping in touch with home through letters, phone calls or visits.

Making new friends at school by being involved in group activities. Managing your time well so that you are able to do all your chores. Manage your finances by using a budget and living within your means.

Learn to resolve conflicts with your parents, siblings, teachers and friends sensibly. Seek help from counselors or friends if need be.

Studying can be made less stressful if:

A You choose a quiet place that is free of distractions to study. The library can be the ideal setting.

B Learn to manage your study time well.

C Learn to take breaks after each hour of study.

D Recognize your limitations and work to improve on your grades.

E Seek help from your teacher or peer when you have challenges in your studies.

F Do not give in to peer pressure to play or while away time instead of reading; the dividend of studying hard is good grades.

G Do not skip classes and hope what you missed will not feature in your examination because you will be examined on what you were taught.

H Do not rely on cramming; rather seek to master a subject by understanding it.

Do not seek escape from stress by doing the following:

A Using Alcohol- Rather than liberating you from stress, creates hangover, fights and traffic violations.

B Using drugs of addiction

C Overwork which causes brain fatigue

D Panic which will disorganize you and make your tension mount

ANOREXIA NERVOSA AND BULIMIA NERVOSA

These are eating disorders arising from mental health instability. Teens with these problems have inordinate preoccupation with food, weight and their appearance.

Anorexia Nervosa

A person with this condition is preoccupied with being thin even though she is thin. The condition is common in adolescent girls and young women; no scientifically established cause of this disorder has been found.

The features of anorexia nervosa include:

A Being underweight for age and height [the person weighs less than 85% of expected weight for her height].

B There is distorted perception for weight in the sense that she thinks she is fat whereas she is very thin.   C She is afraid of weight gain and so indulges in excessive weight control measures such as food restriction, over exercising, vomiting, misuse of laxatives and diuretics [fluid tablets] and diet pills.

D Loss of monthly periods or delay in starting periods in girls.

Bulimia Nervosa

A person with this condition indulges in binge eating followed by induced vomiting or laxative use. Some girls develop bulimia nervosa after recovering from anorexia nervosa. No scientifically established cause of this disease has been found till date.

The features of the condition are as follows:

A Irrational eating followed by guilt feelings

B Excessive measures to prevent weight gain such as fasting, exercising, induced vomiting, misuse of laxatives and diuretics.

C The weight of the person is usually within normal limits or slightly above expected weight.

Consequences of Eating Disorders

The following are the consequences of these disorders:

1 Physically, the person looks frail, haggard with weakened bones [osteoporosis], anaemia and infertility.

2 Psychologically, the person may experience mood swings, depression and an increased tendency towards suicide.

3 Socially, the person feels isolated and would not enjoy the company of people.

4 Emotionally, the person feels guilty for looking haggard and embarrassing her family.

Care of persons with eating disorders

These persons may require Counseling or psychotherapy Dietary education for healthy eating habits

Medication for severe depression Treatment of comorbid conditions arising from the disorder

Nutritional supplementation to hasten recovery.

Family therapy which enables family members give the sick family member the needed support.

Mild cases of eating disorders may be treated from home while severe cases require hospitalization.

Prevention of eating disorders

To prevent eating disorders, teens need good education about healthy eating. Parents should aid their children in developing good self-esteem.

"I cannot think of any need in childhood as strong as the need for a father's protection."

Sigmund Freud

RECOMMENDED PRETEEN AND TEEN IMMUNIZATIONS

The following immunizations can be given to teens and preteens according to the Center for Disease Control Guidelines on immunizations as well as the Advisory Committee on Immunization Practice [ACIP]

1 **Tetanus, Diphtheria toxoids and Acellular Pertussis Vaccine [Tdap]**. It is meant for those aged 11 to 18 years that had completed the recommended DTP/DTap vaccination series and who have not received a tetanus and diphtheria toxoid vaccines [Td] booster for whooping cough. The old pertussis vaccine wears out after 10 years while the new vaccine has fewer side effects and can be used for immunization against reinfection.

Human Papillomavirus Vaccine [HPV]
The first dose is given to girls between 11 and 12 years, second dose is given 2 months after while the third dose is given 6 months after the first dose. Girls between 13 and 18 years who have not been previously

vaccinated can get it. It is the only known vaccine that can prevent cancer; it can prevent cervical cancer in up to 75% of recipients.

3. **Meningococcal Vaccine** It is given to those in ages 11 to 12 years or any unvaccinated teen that is about to enter secondary school or high school.

4 **Influenza [Flu] Vaccine** It is recommended for hospital workers or those at high risk of contacting flu.

5 **Hepatitis A**- It is given to frequent travelers. Two doses are given six months apart.

6 **Hepatitis B** Two doses are given to teens between 11 and 15 years because of high risk activities of youths such as drug use and sexual activity.

7 **Inactivated Poliovirus Vaccine.** Easy international travel with the attending risk of being infected from areas of the world where polio is still present makes it important, though there had been no cases of polio in Western hemisphere since 1987. For all children who got 3 doses of either inactivated polio vaccine [IPV] or oral polio vaccine [OPV] before the age of 4 years, they do not require the 4th dose. If a child got a combination of IPV and OPV, then a fourth dose is required irrespective of the child's current age.

8 **Measles, Mump and Rubella Vaccine [MMR].** 2 doses of the vaccine are given to children at any age who have never had the vaccine before.

9 **Varicella (Chicken Pox) Vaccine.** Two doses are given to unvaccinated children under 13 years at least 3 months apart.

Those aged 13 years and above should get the 2 doses at least 4 weeks apart.

PREVENTING TEENAGE DRUG USE

The following measures would prevent drug use by teenagers:

Have a warm relationship with your child. This would make your child tell you if he/she is considering taking drugs or admit to taking drugs. Help your child cope with the challenges of adolescence and the teenage years. Give the needed support to enable him jettison taking drugs.

Help your child develop zero tolerance for drugs. This can be done as you use drug-related events to harp on the evils of drug addiction.

Help your child develop a sound personal value system. Through moral instructions and constant reading of the Bible, your child will build an impregnable wall against drugs and similar vices.

Know your child's friends and their parents This enables you to have more people watching over your child and encouraging him on the good path.

Help your child choose good friends Bad company corrupts good morals; let your child know the advantages of friends who do not take drugs and how to recognize those who take drugs.

Keep in touch with your child after school hours Through phone calls, text messages and notes keep tab on your child. Know those he hangs out with at these moments.

Get your child engaged in extracurricular activities. Activities like piano lessons or sporting activities use up time that your child could have used for things like drugs.

Be a role model to your child as far as drugs are concerned Let the beauty of not using drugs be evident in your life; let the benefits of sobriety be evident in your life.

A visit to a drug rehabilitation centre may leave a lasting memory of the harmful effects of drugs on your child. When a child sees first hand the wages of drug use, he/she may make a firm decision not to handle drugs.

Ask questions when your teen plans an outing Find out who he/she will be going out with and what they would be doing.

Establish a family tradition of not using drugs Let your child know about healthier ways of enjoying life or handling challenges without recourse to drugs.

Do things together as a family Aside from promoting a keen sense of belonging, it makes a child feel accountable to the family especially as regards proper conduct outside the home.

TEEN SEXUALITY AND HEALTH

Teens must take responsibility for keeping themselves out of harm's way as far as their sexuality is concerned. Sexually transmitted diseases are common and they can cause infertility from damages to the reproductive organs as well as early death if a teen contracts HIV/AIDS.

Sexually transmitted diseases arise from:

Sexual activity at a young age

Having lots of sex partners which amplifies the risk of sexually transmitted diseases

Having unprotected sex-Only latex condoms reduce the risk of sexually transmitted diseases of all the contraceptive devices.

The value of abstinence and virginity pledge

Abstinence is the best preventive measure for sexually transmitted diseases while taking a virginity pledge strengthens a child's resolve to keep sex for marriage.

TEEN LEISURE ACTIVITIES

These are activities that a teen takes delight in and helps him/her relax. Below is a list of some activities that would help a teenager relax

1   Participating in games

2   Watching sporting activities and wrestling

3   Watching movies

Playing video games that require you to think

Going to cinema

Listening to music and dancing

Visiting friends

Traveling to new places

Collecting stamps

IN A NUTSHELL

1   Children and teens have health needs that are peculiar to them such as proper nutrition, exercise, mental fitness etc, etc.

2   Parents should engage their children in such a way that they can promote their health.

3 Immunization schedules should be followed to promote good health.

4 Parents can adopt proactive measures in preventing drug use and sexuality transmitted diseases in their teenagers.

LIFE APPLICATION

1 Do you relate with your child in a way that you can influence him positively on teenage health issues?

2 Do you model good behaviour to your child when it comes to proper nutrition, exercise and self-control?

FURTHER READING

Healthy diet- (1) The Right Choice-Healthy Lifestyle Teenagers[Glasgow Caledonian University] (2) www.amwa-doc.org/publication/WC_Healthbook/dietamwa-ch03.html

1 Haslam D.W., James W.P [2005] Obesity: Lancet 366(9492) :1197-209

2 Swartz, Steven [Nov1, 2007] Obesity. eMedicine.com

3 Stress Management-www.stress.about.com/cs/copingskills/

(4)American Academy of Child and Adolescent Psychiatry website at http://www.aacap.org/page.ww?name=helping+Teenager+With+stress&Section=Facts+For+ families

(5) Kids Health Website at http://www.kidshealth.org/parent/positive/talk/stress_coping.html

6.Eating disorders-http://www.mirror-org/eating dis.html

7. Immunization-http://www.cdc.gov/nip/default.htm

8. The Massachusetts Department of Public Health-www.state.ma.us/dph/cdc/bcdc.htm

PART SEVEN:
DEVELOPING CRITICAL LIFE SKILLS

"Lives of great men all remind us, We can make our lives sublime, And, departing, leave behind us, Footprints on the sand of time."

Henry Wadsworth Longfellow

CHAPTER TWENTY-SIX

Developing the Spirit of Enterprise

FOCUSING QUESTIONS

1. *What is the spirit of enterprise?*

2. *Why does your child need the spirit of enterprise?*

3. *What are the personal qualities that entrepreneurs have in common?*

4. *What is the common set of challenges entrepreneurs face?*

5. *How is the spirit of enterprise developed and sustained?*

THE SPIRIT OF ENTERPRISE

This is the mindset of finding profitable solution to problems facing society. It entails identifying a problem and proffering a solution to it before someone else does. The solution may have commercial value to the inventor. Somebody with this spirit is called an entrepreneur; he habitually creates something of recognized value around perceived opportunities.

WHY YOUR CHILD NEEDS THE SPIRIT OF ENTERPRISE

The following are some reasons: Every child is a rich deposit of talents waiting to be identified and put to good use. It is a spirit of enterprise that is needed to put every talent in a child to profitable use. A spirit of enterprise wipes out poverty from the mind of a child and makes him see boundless opportunities to succeed in life.

1. Increasingly, job opportunities are getting fewer and fewer and we need people who would break out of the mould of seeking employment and create job for themselves and others. The International Labour Organization [ILO] in 2005 made this revelation in 2005 in a report;

"Compared to adults, young people today are more than three times as likely to be unemployed....(and) being without work means being without a chance to work themselves out of poverty. The 4% decrease in the labour market participation rate of young people between 1993 and 2003, which it ascribes to the increase in participation in school, longer time spent in education, generally high unemployed rates, and because many young people dropped out of the labour force as they lost hope of finding work"

A spirit of enterprise would enable your child shape the world around him.

1. Children have very fertile minds and imagination that can be harnessed in developing this spirit. When this mindset is in place, a child will deploy his mind to those aspects of learning that will make him realize set goals.

2. When children's thoughts are gainfully engaged, deviant acts and practices such as peddling and using hard drugs,

smoking and drinking, pornography and sexual promiscuity would hold no attraction for them.

3. We are in an information age where the internet makes knowledge freely available at your finger tips. Knowledge would empower any child to explore whatever field of interest that would enable him realize his dreams.

4. Since like minds flock together, a spirit of enterprise would make your child court the friendship of like minds that would enable him achieve set goals.

5. A spirit of enterprise creates wealth and would deliver your child from the grips of poverty. The wealth and patents created would be passed on to generations yet unborn.

6. The joy of fulfillment that comes from making society better and the recognition that goes with it makes developing the spirit of enterprise a noble venture.

7. Self-employment makes time available for your child to explore and maximize use of the numerous opportunities that would come his way in life.

8. A spirit of enterprise would make your child a role model for the upcoming generation.

"Do not follow where the path may lead---go instead where there is no path and leave a trail."

Unknown

PERSONAL QUALITIES OF MOST ENTREPRENEURS

There are many personal qualities common to outstanding entrepreneurs that you can develop in your child such as:

Entrepreneurs are passionate and highly motivated persons Without this attribute they cannot surmount the challenges that they would encounter every inch of the way. They think big and are focused; this enables them to pursue their dreams with single minded determination.

They are persons of vision Envision what difference your invention will make to society when it is realized. Every important project is birthed in your mind before it becomes reality. Tell your children it is okay to dream and make plans to realize actualize your dreams. Too many young persons go through life without a vision of what they want to become. Without a dream, it is difficult to cash in on an opportunity that will make a difference in a person's life.

They love challenges Get your children to love challenging tasks. Give them assignments that would demand searching for information or interacting with persons who can help them with solution.

They are independent minded Stimulate your child to be unconventional in his thinking. Your child should be trained to have zero tolerance for the status quo; he should be taught to break out of the mould of commonly accepted wisdom.

They love knowledge Entrepreneurs know that knowledge is the wellspring of enterprise. They also know that false limits are set by lack of knowledge. Your child should not only make learning a life long experience but should court the company of knowledgeable people in his field of interest. Henry Ford, the founder of the Ford Motor Company has this to say of the greatest inventor of all times who never had a University education, Thomas Alva Edison, "His knowledge is almost universal, he is interested in every conceivable subject and recognizes no limitation". Ask your child what he has interest in that will be of benefit to society.

Boundless Energy and Irrepressible Spirit Success is the end product of so many failed attempts at realizing a person's dreams. When Thomas Edison's factory caught fire in 1914 and destroyed his phonograph company, he was undeterred. While the buildings were still smoldering he remarked," Although I am 67 years old, I will start all over again tomorrow. We'll build bigger and better than ever. Why should I be downhearted"? Ask your child if he is a writer and his computer crashes with his unprinted manuscript, would he give up or start afresh? Entrepreneurs vaccinate themselves against the effects of repeated failures by having a positive outlook to life.

They have good problem solving skills Entrepreneurs are able to identify societal problems and challenges and ruminate over several options of proffering solutions to these challenges. They gather relevant knowledge as well as interact with persons who can make input into their invention. Ask your child to list five problems that is confronting his environment and let him come up with hypothetical solutions to these problems.

They have good social and communication skills Entrepreneurs at a point in time will work with different set of people to actualize their dream. He will need good social skills that respect people with different or contrary opinions to enable them work together harmoniously. Communication skills are needed to market your ideas to the consuming public.

They are willing to pay the price in terms of acquiring the necessary skills to succeed. If your child needs computer skills to realize his goals, he must acquire these skills from a good source.

They have the ability to handle failure. Entrepreneurship often times can be likened to traveling in an uncharted sea. You will miss your target several times before getting it. An engineer who was at his wits end after so many failed efforts was accosted by Edison. He told Edison, "You know I have been at my problems for months, I have tried every reasonable thing I could think of, and no result, not even a lead". Edison answered, "Reasonable things never work. Thank God, you can't think up any more reasonable things, so you'll have to begin thinking up unreasonable things to try and now you'll hit the solution in no time".

They give back to society Entrepreneurs appreciate the role of society and so they give a lot of their income by way of charity to society. Bill gates, Carnegie and John D Rockefeller are examples of such large hearted persons. They have a high sense of corporate social responsibility.

"Our greatest weakness lies in giving up. The most certain way

to succeed is always to try just one more time"

Thomas Edison

COMMON CHALLENGES THAT ENTREPRENEURS FACE

Getting people to believe in them Common remarks are "This thing has never been done before", "Quit wasting your time and resources", etc.

Getting financial support for your project People are hesitant to support a project that has not been tested in the market.

Getting the right people to work with you Getting people to work with you can be difficult because they may not share your vision.

Getting a market for your products Your products will have to displace existing products in the market for you to get good returns from it.

Lack of persistence in the face of constant trials Those who cannot persist will not know the joy of success.

Competition Entrepreneurs must brace up for stiff competition for products already in existence.

HOW IS THE SPIRIT OF ENTERPRISE DEVELOPED AND SUSTAINED

1. Get appropriate education in your field of interest.

2. Build your self-confidence and self-esteem.

3. Get the needed skills by working in a relevant company.

4. Network with people who share your interest or are working on similar project.

5. Source for finance to bring your products to the market.

6. Never give up on your dreams. Be tenacious. Edison in the 1932 said "Genius is 1% inspiration and 99% perspiration."

7. Let your project be in your area of interest.

8. Dare to be different.

9. Start small but think big; have your head in the clouds but your feet on earth. Know that a journey of a thousand miles starts with a step.

10. Ask for feedback from your customers, it would enable you work to satisfy them.

11. Be innovative; strive to bring in new products always.

12. Learn from your mistakes and aim to be the best in your field of endeavour.

13. Develop the mindset of life long learning; be diversified in your subjects of learning.

IN A NUTSHELL

1. Deep within every child is that innate ability of finding profitable solutions to the problems facing society.

2. A spirit of enterprise when developed in a child brings a harvest of benefits to the child and society.

3. There are some personal qualities common to most entrepreneurs that can be learned or acquired.

4. There are a host of challenges that every entrepreneur must contend with on the path to success.

LIFE APPLICATION

1. What special talents and attributes have you discovered in your child? In what ways can you nurture these gifts to maturity?

2. In what ways do you encourage your child to be all he/she is capable of becoming in life?

FURTIIER READING

Edison: *Wizard of America's Industrial Age.* Babson College Executive Education

Love, J (2005, October 24) *The Entrepreneurial Spirit.* Available at http://www.ezinearticles.com

The Complex Challenges Facing a New Generation of Youths- An Overview of the World Youth Report-Part 1

CHAPTER TWENTY-SEVEN
Developing Thinking Skills

FOCUSING QUESTIONS

1. *Why are thinking skills important?*

2. *What is critical thinking?*

3. *What are the strategies for developing critical thinking skills in your child?*

4. *How can you improve your child's thinking skills?*

IMPORTANCE OF THINKING SKILLS

Thoughts usually govern the actions of a person except when the person acts on the spur of the moment or impulsively. The bible says in Proverbs 23:7, "As a man thinks in his heart, so is he". Your actions are the end products of your thinking pattern.

The goal of teaching is imparting factual information for the student to think about without teaching the student how to think. A child needs to know how to think in order to understand and evaluate the load of information he will be bombarded with all through life.

One of the practical ways of improving your child's thinking skills is through framing your questions in a way that stimulates his thought processes.

Bloom's Taxonomy has broken down human thinking skills into six categories. You can improve your child's thinking skills in each of these categories.

Knowledge, Compression and Application have to do with Concrete thinking skills while Analysis, Synthesis and Evaluation which require more abstraction belong to the realm of Critical thinking skills.

Knowledge This entails remembering what you had read previously and using it to answer questions or shape your life.

Phrases and words such as "How many, define, describe, identify", are helpful in making your child give factual answers while testing his skills in recalling stored information. An example is "How many feet are in a yard of cloth"?

Comprehension This is a test of a child's understanding of the information received. Words such as explain, describe, differentiate are helpful in making your child interpret or translate what he has read. An example is "Explain how a tailor converts a piece of cloth into a dress".

Application This entails using previously learned information to solve a problem. You may frame questions with words like demonstrate, show, examine, etc to make your child apply his knowledge to new situations. An example is "What is the similarity in making a dress and sewing a curtain"?

Analysis The child is made to break down a piece of information in order to discover the connectedness of different parts of the information. Frame the questions with words like Explain, analyze, compare, classify, arrange, etc. An example is "Explain the difference between a custom made dress and a dress bought at a shop?"

Synthesis Here prior knowledge and skill are combined to create something new. Use words or phrases such as create, design, what if, etc. to make your child create something new. For example "How would a tailor design a dress from jute?"

Evaluation A child is made to judge or decide according to some available information whether an exercise was rightly or wrongly done. Use words like assess, discuss, measure, compare, select summarize to make your child pass judgment on an exercise. For example "Are custom made dresses better than factory made dresses?"

"Perhaps the most valuable result of all education is the ability to make yourself do the thing you have to do, when it ought to be done whether you like it or not."

Thomas Huxley

CRITICAL THINKING

Critical thinking is reasonable, reflective, responsible and skillful thinking that empowers a person to decide on what to believe or do. It is also a non-linear, open-ended and complex thinking pattern that enables a person have multiple answers to a question, have different perspectives and give different interpretations to situations. Such a way of thinking would make a person ask the right questions, gather relevant information, creatively sift the information

and reason with the information to reach conclusions about what needs to be done.

It is a higher thinking needed for considering weighty issues of life such as serving on a murder trial jury or choosing which political candidate to support after reviewing their manifestoes. It is one skill that enables a person create order from the seemingly chaotic world we are in.

Children are not born with the power to think critically, neither can they develop this ability on their own; they must be taught. Math and science instructors have these information and skills because it is an integral part of their learning.

Critical thinking is scientific thinking applied by ordinary people to understand natural phenomenon. It enables a person to think for one's self and to make those decisions that affect one's life.

THE VALUE OF CRITICAL THINKING

It empowers you to think for yourself. Most people rely on others to think for them; they would rather indulge in wishful, hopeful and emotional thinking, hoping that what they believe is true because they wish it to be so.

It enables you to identify problems. Critical thinking will make you gather relevant information about a problem, analyze the information and arrive at conclusion and what needs to be done independently.

It enables you to face objective reality. You do this by gaining reliable knowledge on contemporary issues.

"There's nothing that can help you understand your beliefs more than trying to explain them to an inquisitive child."

Frank A. Clark

STRATEGIES FOR DEVELOPING CRITICAL THINKING SKILLS IN YOUR CHILD

You may employ the following strategies in teaching your child critical thinking:

Ask your child question that does not have a specific answer in an informal setting. If your child plays electronic football with his play station [Computer video game], ask him how the producers of the software can make it more exciting. Ask him how he can be as successful in real life football game as he is on the screen?

The personality and interests of your child are windows into how your child's mind works. Interact with your child on this basis and teach him critical thinking. Watch him when he is at play and determine the level of complexity in thinking he displays in his plays. Does he compare or discuss different computer games in terms of their complexities, does he engage in the analysis of societal problems with his mates?

Ask your child philosophical questions such as why there is so much evil in this world Listen to his answers and assess how much of critical thinking he deploys in coming to his conclusions. Would he require your help in upgrading his critical thinking skills

Demonstrate critical thinking by pondering aloud your frustrations about your country's social problems. Let him hear you talk about what you would do to combat corruption and infrastructural decay in Nigeria if you ever become the President of this great country.

Take him along to public lectures such as Inaugural lectures or Colloquia or Political debates. He will learn to listen to a lecture actively rather than passively. When he responds correctly to questions related to the lecture, it shows he listened actively; through questions you can evaluate his power of analysis. Ask him the situations he can apply his new knowledge to. Ask your child after listening to a talk or message, one significant thing he learned and one thing he is confused about from the lecture.

Discourage your child from being mere receivers of information. Encourage him to talk about and trust his own thoughts about any subject matter after he has thought deeply and made researches about the issue at hand. In this way he will realize the importance of ideas especially when they have connection with recognize patterns. Let your child know the importance of ideas because ideas rule the world.

Get him to take his home work seriously. Home work is meant to stimulate your child's reasoning and equip him with the ability to source for information to answer questions.

Home works that contain questions which students are required to answer force them to organize their thoughts and think critically about the information they have sourced. In this way, they are able to compose concise, logically persuasive line of reasoning about why they reached a particular conclusion.

Quantitative reasoning and word problems in mathematics enhance critical thinking skills. Subjects like mathematics, physics and chemistry that require solutions to mathematical problems invariably teach critical thinking in the cause of the curriculum. Problem solving skills are intertwined with critical thinking.

Essay writing or long term papers. Writing is easily the best way to teach your child critical thinking skills because the child is compelled to organize his thoughts, think about the topic, gather data in a logical way and conclude his write up in a persuasive manner. Good writing is a good judge of a person's critical thinking skills.

Performance of simple experiments. This exposes your child to scientific reasoning in the course of explaining the result of his experiments.

Engagement in self-directed learning You may ask your child to write a paper on a topic like the planetary system which he has not been taught at school. If he succeeds at this task, he would have learned firsthand what it means to be responsible for his own learning since he would have sifted through a lot of information to write the paper. This is a good way of developing critical thinking.

Get your child to understand the difference between reasoning and rationalization. Reasoning is rigorous mental activity that involves evaluation of facts as against rationalization which is merely giving excuses for a particular position that cannot be justified by facts.

Teach your child how to argue with facts. He must learn how to strip an argument of irrelevancies while phrasing it in its salient terms. He must learn to use evidence skillfully and impartially in debates or writing.

Teach your child how to form opinions. This must come from critically evaluating the facts at hand. He must be aware that his opinion may be wrong, flawed, biased or illogical as a result of personal preferences. It is good to respect other people's opinions even when they are at variance with yours.

In a Nutshell

School gives a "child what to think" about in the form of lectures while learning "how to think" is the way to understanding and evaluating any body of information. Children need to be taught how to think so that they can overcome any limitations put on their learning horizon by their teachers and parents.

Critical thinking is valuable in all spheres of a child's life and so must be nurtured in a child if he is to succeed in life.

Life Application

1. Plan to attend a public lecture with your teenage children with the goal of evaluating their thinking skills. Ask them questions relating to the lecture.

2. How can you make your child employ critical thinking skills in everyday life without prompting from you?

Further Reading

Council for Exceptional Children: *Improving Your Child's Thinking Skills.*

Available at http://www.familyeducation.com

Shaunessy, E. (Summer 2006) *Enhancing Critical-Thinking Skills in Children: Tips for Parents.* Duke Gifted Letter. Volume 6, Issue 4.

Duke University Talent Identification Program http://www.dukegiftedletter.com

Schafersman D.S. [January, 1991] *An Introduction to Critical Thinking*

Statkiewicz W.R., Allen R.D. [1983] *Practical Exercises to Develop Critical Thinking Skills.* Journal of College Science Teaching vol. 12, p. 262-266

Fischer A. *Critical thinking.* Cambridge University Press, 2002

Critical Thinking Core Concepts hosted by Laureen Miller and Michael Connelly at http://www.kcmetro.cc.mo.us/longview/ctac/corcnotes.htm

Chapter Twenty-Eight
Decision-Making Skills

Focusing Questions

1. *What is the importance of decision making skills?*
2. *What challenges do teenagers face in making decisions?*
3. *What are the critical steps in making decisions?*
4. *How can a father guide his children in developing decision making skills?*
5. *How can you help your child improve on his/her decision making skills?*
6. *What are some common but important issues that teenagers make decisions about?*

Decision-Making Skills

So much of life is about making choices; choices are the end stages of a person's decision making process. Some persons are masters of prevarication because of their chronic inability to make up their minds about what decisions to make. Children from teenage years must develop this skill if they are to make good choices in life. In a single day, the decision a teenager would make ranges from what to read, where to go, which invitation to honour to how long to watch the TV or surf the net etc.

The Importance of Decision Making Skills in Teenagers

It is an evidence of a maturing person One of the proofs of maturity is being able to make responsible decisions on your own.

Evidence of independence from parents Part of the duty of parents is to prepare their children for a life on their own. Children who have developed this skill cope better in a world filled with choices to make.

A teenager's choice to drive after drinking may have consequences that affect others A teenager who drives a car after a drinking binge can destroy himself and others in a car crash arising from his drunken state.

Adds value to a person's life Persons who make up their minds quickly on issues are less boring than those who spend ages doing so. They are more attractive personalities to deal with.

It plays a protective role Teenagers who have decided against taking drugs or indulging in youth vices such as pornography resist any pressure to go against their will when they are challenged. Good decision making skills would insure a teenager against risky behaviour.

It delivers from peer pressure Youths respect their peers who have made up their minds on certain issues and would not go contrary to their decision no matter the pressures they come under.

It gives a person identity By constantly saying no to certain vices, a teenager comes to be known for his/her stand on some issues. Your mates know what you can do and what you are unlikely to do. You are not carried around by the latest fad in town because of the self-regulation that good decision making skills bequeath to a person.

Gives happiness and fewer frustrations in life You are a happier person for controlling your life rather than have your friends control you. You do what you believe in; therefore you have fewer frustrations in life. Suicidal thoughts do not haunt you because you are a happy person.

You are a more productive person In all you do; you have a head start because you have already resolved on a line of action.

You save time by making a decision You do not keep people waiting when you decide on what to do.

Employability People who have good decision making skills are the toast of employers because they inspire others at the place of work and are usually very productive at the work place. Most industrialized and emerging economies require workers that are making decisions at higher levels of sophistication than preceding generations; they value people who can think critically about diverse issues and make the right decisions [Laskey & Campbell, 1991].

Leadership potential Good decision making skills mark you out as a potential leader because others are willing to follow you. You are able to achieve production targets in the company because of this skill.

"Twenty years from now you will be more disappointed by the things that you didn't do than by the ones you did do. So throw off the bowlines. Sail away from the safe harbor. Catch the trade winds in your sails. Explore. Dream. Discover".

Mark Twain

CHALLENGES TEENAGERS FACE IN MAKING GOOD DECISIONS

They are limited by experience and knowledge. Lack of knowledge and experience about life may limit the options open to teenagers when it comes to making the right decision. They may only see "either or" choices rather than a host of options to pick from or consider [Fischhoff et al., 1999]

Youthful exuberance Teenagers may be overwhelmed by emotions and fail to use appropriate decision making process in tackling issues.

Poor parent-child relationship When interaction between parent and child is not constructive, teenagers do not consider their parents credible enough to depend on when it comes to decision making.

Paucity of Mentors In an increasingly decadent society such as ours, teenagers need mentors who will live out the value of making good choices in life. When such mentors are few, teens are deprived of these role models.

Poor judgment They may perceive certain behaviours as less risky or may be overly optimistic about their ability to recognize and avoid life threatening situations [Cohn, Macfarlane, Yanez, & Imai, 1995].

Consideration of the opinions of their peers This may make them throw caution to the wind in taking decisions that have bad consequences.

Banking on their own experience They may choose to bank on their limited experience in determining the probability of the negative consequences of their actions catching up on them. Lack of experience may not enable teens to accurately estimate the probability of negative consequences

Judging the credibility of Internet information. Information overload emanating from the net often confuses teenagers. Teenagers often are not able to sift wheat from chaff present in the deluge of information that the internet presents. Immaturity coupled with ignorance will deny teenagers the benefit of accurate information when making important decisions

Pervasive media influence The media may trivialize certain issues that have dangerous repercussions that only discerning minds can escape.

CRITICAL STEPS IN DECISION-MAKING PROCESS

In real life, we often have to make decisions on the spur of the moment without enough time to go through all the listed steps below, however when you have developed this skill to some extent, it enables you make quick and proper decisions.

The following are the critical steps in making a decision:

1. Identify the specific issue on which you want to make a decision. It may relate to choosing a particular person as a friend, ending a relationship or choosing to delay engaging in sexual activity till marriage.

2. List the relevant choices open to you.

3. Gather relevant information on the choices you have to make.

4. Decide on what yardstick to use in judging each choice.

5. List the consequences of each choice you may decide to make.

6. Assess the likelihood of each consequence actually coming to pass.

7. Determine the significance of each of these consequences.

8. Determine the best of the alternatives to follow after combining all the information available to you.

9. Put the decision into action. Execute your plan by transforming your decision into a specific plan of action steps.

10. Evaluate the outcome of your decision. Are there lessons to be learnt from your decision on this issue? This will help in developing your decision-making skills.

PRACTICAL STEPS TO HELPING YOUR CHILD MAKE DECISIONS

As a father, you would be doing your child a world of good as you help him/her develop decision-making skills in the following way:

Prepare yourself to let go of your child as far as decision-making is concerned. You have always made decisions for him. Now is the time to see him make decisions beginning with decisions on the little issues of life.

Let your child choose an issue on which he wants to make a decision on. Ask him to list the available options.

Ask him to think through the options. Give him enough time to think through the options.

Allow him to make the decision by himself. Evaluate the decision your child has made with him. Do not be judgmental while doing this. If the outcome is not what he hoped for, tell him that it is part of our limitations as human beings and secondly it is the reason for always being careful when you have to make decisions. Discuss with him how he could have done things differently to achieve a better result. Praise him for the effort and let him know that experience is borne out of such efforts.

HOW TO HELP YOUR CHILD IMPROVE ON HIS DECISION-MAKING SKILLS

Encourage your child to make decisions whenever the need arises rather than looking up to you or following peer decision. A child grows in his ability to make decisions by making decisions. Providing opportunities for making decisions helps your child's decision making skills.

Teach your child how his emotions may influence his thinking and behaviour so that he would exercise due care in making decisions.

Providing your child with the real accurate statistics of the actual number of young persons engaging in risky behaviour would help in counteracting the hype in media messages [Fishhoff et al, 1999].

Involving your child in family decisions makes him gain experience from you

When you use concrete situations like teenage pregnancy that reflect young people's interests and have relevance to their lives to illustrate the importance of good decisions, he is bound to exercise due care [Campbell and Laskey, 1991].

Helping your child recognize his biases can affect him in making decisions will make him take decision-making seriously.

When your child knows how his decision will affect others, he will choose to make good decisions.

"The father of the righteous shall greatly rejoice: and he that begetteth a wise child shall have joy of him."

Proverbs 23:24

COMMON ISSUES THAT TEENAGERS MAKE DECISIONS ABOUT

Decision to always obey parents. When a child makes this decision, he is spared the consequences of bad decisions because parents in most instances have the best interest of their child at heart.

1. **Decision to be law abiding.** Such a decision would make the child abide by school rules and the laws of society. He would not be involved in criminal activities that can lead to imprisonment

2. **Decision to excel in academics** This would mean more time for reading and less time for play and frivolities.

3. **Decision to delay sexual activities till after marriage** This will remove the fear

of sexually transmitted diseases, teenage pregnancy and the need for contraception. It will make more time available for developing platonic relationships.

4. **Decision not to drink alcohol, smoke or use hard drugs**. This will protect him from the long arms of the law as well as the company of delinquent youths whose stock-in-trade is these vices.

5. **Decision not to engage in violent behaviour**. This will make him shun violent films and the company of persons who love violence.

6. **Decision to be modest in dressing**. Females who make this decision are particular about the type of dresses they wear. They chose to dress modestly rather than provocatively. Teenage boys choose to dress like respectable gentleman rather than Motor Park touts.

7. **Decision on choice of friends.** When you choose friends who share the same goals with you, you mutually reinforce each other in your goals.

8. **Decision on which career to pursue**. This will come from realistically appraising your interest and your abilities together with the opportunities you how to study for your career.

9. **Decision on which University to attend**. This depends on whether the University has a programme of your choice and also if you can afford the tuition.

IN A NUTSHELL

1. Decision making skills are very important in teenagers' lives because of the many choices they have to make on their own on issues that can greatly affect their lives.

When a father models good decision making skills to a son, it becomes easy for the child to develop this vital skill.

2. There are many practical ways by which a father can help impart this skill to his child.

LIFE APPLICATION

1. How would you rate your child's decision making skills? Does he think through issues before making decision or he acts on the spur of the moment?

2. Do you involve your child in making decisions affecting him or you simply decide for him on most issues? Are you preparing him for a life without you or you always consider him too young to decide on his own on most issues?

3. With your knowledge of your child, which practical ways will you adopt to enhance his decision making skills?

FURTHER READING

Brockman M. S., Russell T. S., *Decision-Making/Reasoning Skills.*

Russo J.E., Schoemaker, P., *Winning Decisions: Getting it Right the First Time.* Doubleday 2001

Lewis H.W. *Why Flip a Coin? The Art and Science of Good Decisions.* Wiley, 1998

Susan Jeffers., *Feel the Fear but Do It Anyway.* Harcourt, Brace,New York, 1987

Paulena Nickell, Ann Smith, and Suzanne P. Tucker; *Management in Family Living.* John Wiley and Sons, New York, 1976.

CHAPTER TWENTY-NINE
Problem-Solving Skills

FOCUSING QUESTIONS

1. *What is the importance of problem-solving skills?*

2. *What are the steps in problem-solving?*

3. *What are some problems common to teenagers?*

4. *How can you help your child develop problem-solving skills?*

THE IMPORTANCE OF PROBLEM-SOLVING SKILLS

Problems are obstacles or challenges on the path to self-fulfillment or self-actualization. The only child that never needed a problem-solving skill was the child borne dead on arrival [A still birth]. Life is full of problems; the extent to which we are able to surmount problems is the extent to which society rates us as successful. The problems of children vary according to their ages. Children need the experience and maturity of their fathers to see them through the mine-field that the present day world has become. Unresolved problems and issues are the root causes of a significant percentage of mental illnesses because they cause sustained stress. A person is described as mature when he has the right attitude to handling problems. Some persons use the mental process of denial to escape from their problems while others simply wish problems away. The ability to foresee a problem and prepare to solve it on your own terms makes you a mature person. Problem-solving skills are needed by young persons if they are to live a life of their own, independent of their parents.

"There are not seven wonders of the world in the eyes of a child. There are seven million."

Walt Streightiff

CASE STUDY

Ralph did not pass English language at credit level when he sat for the Senior Secondary School Certificate Examination in 2002; a key requirement for admission in to the University for any degree programme. Rather than making another attempt at passing English language, he chose to enter a College of Education for a 3-year National Certificate for Education [NCE] programme which he successfully completed. For now, he can teach and earn a living but has no prospects for further education unless he obtained a pass in English language at credit level. Presently, NCE is the minimum entry level qualification for teaching, however if a University degree becomes the minimum qualification for teaching in future, he would be without a job. He is torn between getting a job to make life more comfortable or going back to re-write his English language paper so that he would have a secure future. Obviously, he has a problem on hand, how would he go about this?

STEPS TO SOLVING PROBLEMS

The following steps may be adopted for solving problems:

Put a name to the problem This will guide you in seeking information about the problem. From our case study above, Ralph has a problem with English language and needs to pass it at credit level for him to further his education.

Analyze the problem and gather as much helpful information on the subject as you can. Ralph finds it more convenient to speak vernacular with his peers than English because English is not his mother tongue. However, one of the best ways of mastering English is by speaking it so that your grammatical errors can be noticed and corrected. He will need to motivate himself now to speak English more often than he is used to.

Break the problem into smaller units that can be better managed The different aspects of English language such as English grammar, comprehension, words and their meanings, synonyms and antonyms, essay writing, English lexis and structure, oral English, etc must be mastered by Ralph if he is to have a good chance of passing the subject at his next attempt.

List the possible solutions to the problem It is good to list the possible solutions to the problem while analyzing each on its own merits. Ralph has the following options:

1. Going back to senior secondary school for a whole year of classes. Not an attractive offer since he has his NCE already.

2. Taking tutorial lessons in English language to prepare him better. This is a good option, however it costs money.

3. Reading fiction and non-fiction books to enlarge his vocabulary and essay writing skills. This requires determination.

4. Reading newspapers especially editorials where he can note words that are strange to him and which he can look up in the dictionary. He can go to the library for newspapers if he cannot afford to buy his own copies

5. Listening to radio especially British Broadcasting Corporation and Voice of American which have English learning programmes.

Choose the option(s) that suit (s) you most and act on it [them]. Ralph may choose all of the above except the very first option on the list.

Evaluation and analysis of the result Find out if the measures you are taking are producing good results. Ralph will need regular assessment tests from his tutorial teachers to know if his preparations are adequate for him to pass his next English Examination.

"Being a father is something mythical and infinitely important: a protector, who would keep a lid on all the chaotic and catastrophic possibilities of life."

Tom Wolfe

SOME TOOLS USED IN PROBLEM-SOLVING

Consultation-Ask those who have experience on the issue or are professionals in the field about the problem you are facing.

Internet Use the internet to gather information on the subject.

Brain storming Work with a team and pool their ideas to come up with a solution to the problem.

Use the Root Cause Analysis Find the fundamental cause of the problem. Ask as many "whys" to get to the root of the problem.

Use a flow chart List all the possible steps in solving the problem. Now address each step and follow the leads.

SOME PROBLEMS COMMON TO TEENAGERS

The following are some problems common to teenagers:

1. Disobedience to parents and constituted authorities
2. Breaking of school rule
3. Low self-esteem
4. Bullying-either as a victim or a perpetrator
5. Low academic grades
6. Poor reading habits
7. Behavioural problems such as violent temper
8. Lateness to school and occasions
9. Pornography
10. Drinking Alcohol
11. Smoking
12. Premarital sex
13. Stealing
14. Telling lies
15. Poor study habits, failure to turn in assignments
16. Shyness
17. Untidiness
18. Procrastination'
19. Keeping bad company
20. Examination Malpractice
21. Poor Money management
22. Poor communication skills

23. Poor interpersonal skills

24. Vulgarity - Use of swear words

25. Bed Wetting

26. Time wasting

How To Help Your Child Develop Problem Solving Skills

1. Let your child know you are available to help him develop this skill.

2. When there is a problem, listen to him present the problem.

3. Ask him the possible options he wants to explore.

4. Tell him to come up with an action plan.

5. Make input if necessary.

6. Let him execute the plan.

7. Review the outcome with him and praise him for the effort.

In A Nutshell

1. Teenagers face many problems as they transit from childhood to youth. Identifying problems and ways of solving them are signals that a child is developing properly.

2. A child should be taught the various ways of solving problems.

3. A child's ability to solve problems increases the more of his personal problems he is able to solve using the above techniques.

Life Application

1. Make a list of the problems your child is grappling with that you can help him solve.

2. What personal problem do you have at hand that you can use to model problem-solving skill to your child?

Further Reading

Anderson, J.R., Boyle, C.B, Reiser, B. J. (1988): *Intelligent Tutoring Systems.* Science 228:456-462

Anzai, K., Simon, H.A (1979). *The Theory of Learning by Doing.* Psychological Review 81:124-140

Mayer R.E (1992) *Thinking Problem Solving, Cognition* 2nd Edition New York: Freeman and Company

McNamara C. *Basic Guidelines to Problem Solving and Decision Making.* Available at http://www.mapnp.org/library/prsn_prd_bsc.htm

Chapter Thirty

Helping Your Child Choose a Career

Focusing Questions

1. Why is your child's career choice an important issue?

2. What are the parents' roles in career development and vocational choice?

3. What are some common misconceptions about choosing your career?

4. How can you help your child choose the right career when he/she has no idea of what to do?

5. What is career development process?

6. What are some common careers your child can choose from?

Importance of Choosing the Right Career

There have been cases of highly trained professionals such as medical doctors and lawyers who left their professions later in life to pursue careers in fashion designing or running a bakery. Such professionals would tell you their hearts had always been in their new found occupation. What could be the possible reasons for this problem?

Firstly, a teenager out of youthful exuberance might choose a career, he knows very little about only to find out later in life that he made the wrong choice and then decides to opt out.

Secondly, a child might choose a career just to please the father or mother; later in life when he wants to please himself, he may make a career switch.

Thirdly, a child may choose a career because that career matches his academic ability without any recourse to his interest in the career

Fourthly, peer pressure might make a child choose a career he would later abandon because he wanted to please his peers. Fifthly, many parents view career choice as an area that is out of their control and in which their input may not be needed.

Sixthly, some parents see career choice as a trial and error matter that their child can experience for himself.

Parents have a lot to offer when it comes to intervening in their children's lives so that they can choose a career that they would be happy with for the rest of their lives. Parents are influential figures with whom whether deliberately or unintentionally, children become aware of and are exposed to different occupations or career opportunities and implied expectation.

"Everyman is rich who has a child to love and guide."

Unknown

PARENTS' ROLES IN CAREER DEVELOPMENT AND VOCATIONAL CHOICE

Parents' role in career development and vocational choice are important for the following reasons:

Parental approval aids career choice Teenagers need their parents' approval to consider and explore any career. They are unsure of themselves and so believe their parents are more knowledgeable about different careers. Teenagers' aspirations or expectations are influenced by their parents' aspirations or expectations for them; they have higher aspirations for themselves when they know their parents aspiration for them. They also believe since their parents would be financially involved in their training, it is good for them to be part of the decision making process. It boosts their confidence when they have their parents input in to their career choice. Different studies have found that many college or University students cite parents as an important influence on their choice of career [Knowles, 1998; Majoribanks, 1997; Mau and Bikos, 2000; Smith 1991; Wilson and Wilson, 1992].

Watch your utterances about different careers Parental messages may contain an underlying message such as "don't make the same mistake that I made" in making some children rule out certain careers. A teacher who does not like teaching may make remarks about teaching that would make his child not consider teaching as a career option. Such remarks will make teenagers select specific courses or pursue other occupations.

Parents Education and Income Educated and high income parents have high career expectations for their children [Trice, 1991]. They are more knowledgeable about different professions as well as have the financial wherewithal to train their children. By virtue of their social circle, some low paying careers automatically fall into an exclusion list for their children.

Family Business A child born in to a family with established businesses will likely choose a career that will make him useful in the family business[Guerra and Braungart-Rieker, 1999; Lankard, 1995; Mickelson and Volasco, 1998; Otto, 2000; Mau, Hitchcock and Calvert, 1998]

Father's Occupational Status A father's occupation has a strong correlation with his son's occupation [Blau 1992; Blau and Duncan, 1967; Conroy, 1997]. Many sons take after their father's profession because they see their father as their role model.

Family size Large families have less money to aid the older children in their educational pursuits. Once the older children leave home, the younger ones may receive more financial assistance to pursue more lucrative careers [Schulenberg et al 1984, Downey, 1995].

> **"Many children have gone further than they thought they could because a parent knew they could."**
>
> Unknown

SOME COMMON MISCONCEPTIONS ABOUT CHOOSING A CAREER

The following are some misconceptions about career choice;

You can be happy with just any career. Nothing can be further from the truth. Happiness in a career derives from the fulfillment you derive from it, the remuneration you get from it as well as your future prospects in the career.

Making a career choice is easy. Making the right career choice is not easy because you have to go through a process that includes self-assessment, career exploration, making a decision and following your career plan.

The most popular career is what you need to go for. Every now and again, a list of the "most sought after' career comes out. Going for the most popular career does not guarantee happiness or success in that career. Follow the career development process to arrive at what is best for you.

1. **Somebody else can make a career decision for you**. A career counselor or your teacher can guide you in your choice of career but ultimately, you will have to make a choice. When you make a career decision yourself, you will not shift blames when challenges arise in course of training for the career.

2. **Your choice of career can make a success of you**. You are the one that will give value to any particular career you choose. It's your personal attributes that define your career. It is what you put in building a career that determines your level of success in that career.

3. **It is impossible to make a career out of my hobby**. Whatever you derive joy from doing can actually be a career if you can turn it in to an income generating venture.

4. **A career decision is a permanent one**. You can always change your mind about a career once you feel your career prospects are bleak. You must be willing to acquire the necessary skills for the new career.

5. **A career with good pay will make you happy**. Money alone cannot bring career happiness. You need self-fulfillment and prospects of career advancement to make you happy.

6. **Because my uncle is happy with his career, I will be happy if I chose the same career**. You are very different from your uncle; you may not share the same priorities in life. Follow the career development process for every career under your consideration to find out what is best for you.

7. **My skills will become redundant once I switch my career**. Your skills are a permanent part of you once you acquire them; you can adapt them to fit in to your new career.

8. **I need a work experience in a particular career before I can choose it**. No, you do not need a work experience. You can read about any career or occupation on the internet for you to make an informed decision about it.

9. **All I need to succeed is to land a good career**. You need hard work and continual updating of skills and knowledge to make good success of most careers.

STRATEGIES FOR HELPING YOUR CHILD MAKE A CAREER CHOICE

The following strategies would help you prepare your child for a good career choice:

Build and maintain an open relationship with your child. Your level of support, guidance and responsiveness in his academic challenges would make him open to your ideas on career choice. Your child will accept what you say about any profession as the truth and may not bother to prove its validity because he believes you have his best interest at heart. Be constructively involved in your child's career interest in ways that can continually further his career development and learning.

1. **Build and maintain an open relationship with your child's teachers and school counselor.** Sound their opinion about your child's career interests and consider whatsoever advice given.

2. **Help your child meet the challenges of adolescent years by gradually giving him room to make personal decisions.** When a child's decision-making skills are well honed, he will confidently choose a career of his choice.

3. **Be involved in the Parent Teachers Association of your child's school.** This gives you firsthand knowledge of your child's school environment and enables you to judge it's suitability in enabling your child meet the educational requirement for the pursuit of his choice career.

4. **Help your child identify opportunities in fields of work that give him insider knowledge of his career of interest.** If your child wants to study medicine, help him get an opportunity to spend a day with a doctor in his clinic so that he can have a feel of a doctor's work.

5. **Help your child match interests, skills and values with possible future work options.** You are in a better position to dispassionately match your child's abilities with his interests and give advice accordingly.

6. **Assist your child research all possible routes to achieving his career dream.** Download articles from the net on different careers for your child to peruse; help your child secure opportunities to interview different personalities in his career of interest.

7. **Help your child understand that a career is a journey not a destination.** The aphorism of a "journey of a thousand miles begins with a step" aptly describes what it takes to build a successful career.

CAREER DEVELOPMENT PROCESS

This is an established pathway for making an informed decision on which career to follow; a father may well painstakingly go through the process with his child to prepare him adequately before making a committal to any career. The process can be reduced to four steps:

STEP ONE: SELF-ASSESSMENT

You need to understand yourself in the following contexts:

1. Your likes and dislikes, your personal attributes and your character qualities.

2. Your temperament. If you delight in working alone with machines and computers and hate the company of people, you may not be carved out for a career in the health care industry. A career in engineering may well suit you.

3. Your abilities and aptitudes must match the requirements for the career of your choice; you cannot hate mathematics

and yet dream of being an electrical engineer.

4. Strength and weaknesses must put you in good stead in your career of choice.

5. Your attitudes must conform to what is required in your career of choice.

6. Your interests should not suffer on account of your chosen profession; a person with strong interests in building a family should not consider a career that occupies him for fifteen hours a day.

7. Your life and personal values must conform to the demands of your career of choice.

STEP TWO: EXPLORATION

This is the stage when you take more steps to find out in greater details what the career of your choice demands.

1. Make a list of occupations to explore; a list of 5 to 10 occupations may be adequate. Occupational clusters may include Healthcare industry which encompasses Medicine, Pharmacy, Nursing, Laboratory Science, Physiotherapy, Radiotherapy, Medical Records etc.

2. Educational and training options in Vocational/Technical/College/University

3. The effect of the career on your family, belief/faith

STEP THREE: DECISION MAKING

1. Before making up your mind, you need to do more detailed research on your narrowed down options regarding what best suits you.

2. The need for informational interviewing may be there; you interview professionals in your choice career especially on some aspects you need clarifications about.

3. Job shadowing-here you spend some time with a professional in your career of choice at his place of work so that you can observe at a close range what it takes to be in that career.

4. Externship/Internship-You spend some time working in that career to have a first hand experience of the job.

5. Part time work in a related industry.

6. Volunteer work in a related industry.

STEP FOUR: TAKE ACTION

1. Confirm your career choice with a qualified counselor.

2. Train for your career and acquire the necessary skill.

A LIST OF CAREER CHOICES

A Persons who like working with their hands would like careers in:

Electrical Engineering
Agriculture
Electronics Engineering Aquaculture
Computer Engineering
Architecture
Civil Engineering
Estate valuing
Building
Quantity Surveying
Marine Engineering
Aviation
Petroleum Engineering
Computer Science
Chemical Engineering
Metallurgy
Aeronautic Engineering

Information Technology
Mechanical Engineering
Mining Engineering
Instrumentation Engineering Robotics
Textile Engineering

B Persons who like investigations, who are inquisitive and self-confident, might like a career in:

Law
Anthropology
Cyber Law
Archaeology
Marine Law
Biotechnology
Laboratory science
Biochemistry
Journalism
Criminology
Military
Food Processing
Police Force
Pilot
Forensic Medicine

C Persons who love interacting with people, listening to them and offering help;

Medicine
Human Resources Management
Dentistry
Public Relations
Physical Therapy
Fitness Instructor
Homeopathic Medicine
Political Science/Politics
Teaching
Mass Communication
Guidance Counseling
Motivational Speaking
Clergy/Ministry
Nursing

Nutrition and Dietetics
Veterinary Science

D Creative persons who love expressing themselves in imaginative and unconventional ways using words, music, painting etc

Artists Beauticians
Fine Artists
Fashion Design
Writing
Modeling
Drama
Interior Decoration
Music/Composer
Photography
Film Production/Directing
Travel & Tourism
Cinematography
Printing and Publishing

E Persons with a flair for business who have entrepreneurial spirit, who love working with figures and data:

Accountancy
Hospital Management & Administration
Banking and Finance
Hotel and Hospitality Management
Insurance
Statistics
Marketing
Civil Service
Business Management
Events Management
Secretarial Services

IN A NUTSHELL

1. Parents have a lot to offer when it comes to their child's career choice because the child gets to know of different careers through their parents. Parental

endorsement of a child's career boosts the child's confidence about him.

2. Teenagers have some misconceptions about career choice that should be addressed to enable them make the right choices.

3. There are many strategies you can adopt to guide your child in his or her career choice.

4. Painstakingly taking your child through a career development process helps him or her make an informed decision on what career to pursue in life.

LIFE APPLICATION

1. Are your feelings about your career positive enough to make your child follow in your footsteps career-wise?

2. Would you want to follow the career development process in helping your child choose his or career?

FURTHER READING

What Color is Your Parachute? Ten Speed Press, 2001

Paul Phifer, *College Majors and Careers: A Resource Guide for Effective Life Planning.* Ferguson, 2000

University of Waterloo online Career Development Manual available at http://www.adm.uwaterloo.ca/infocecs/CRC/manual-home.html

A Guide to Choosing a Major available at http://www.wesleyan.edu/deans/sophmajor.html